THE SCIENCE OF MEDITATION

SNEH CHAKRABURTTY

New Age Books

ISBN: 978-81-7822-322-3 (Indian)

ISBN: 0-9730057-2-6 (Canadian)

First Edition: Delhi, 2009

Published by

New Age Books

A-44 Naraina Industrial Area Phase I

New Delhi-110028 (India)

Email: nab@vsnl.in

Website: www.newagebooksindia.com

Printed in India

at Shri Jainendra Press

A-45 Naraina Phase-I, New Delhi-110028

THE SCIENCE OF MEDITATION

Man has to learn, understand and, finally, recognise obvious Nature as the Great Mother, who will reveal Her secrets and the inherent *dharma.* Armed with this insight, Man can gain the Supreme Knowledge, the only kind worthy, and be able to rise above shallow intellectualism.

Dedicated to the Master Swami Chinmayananda

Appreciation is felt for my husband
Joti Chandra Chakraburtty and my friend Carolyn Gray
for suggestions during its writing

Preface

Soul Culture... And it's base – the Yoga of Meditation. That's what the Master, Swami Chinmayananda, taught me, and many others like me. For Soul Realisation, the Yoga of Meditation is the highest technique of self-unfoldment. It has its roots in the search to find God and, therefore, to fulfill Life's commitment. It involves uniting Man with everything, animate and inanimate... plant, animal, even stone. It is about being One with the Earth and, eventually, being One with the universe by finding out a Cosmic Connection.

This unity needs, first, raising Man to a higher state of congeniality – a physical, mental and intellectual metamorphosis that restores one to perfect health. Once complete, Man can develop patience and perseverance within himself, and an implicit trust in all his endeavours. Man can, then, approach Nature with transformed intuitive knowledge, and cherish and care for Her... For everything is within Her and She is in everything.

Inherent laws govern Creation, particularly the 'lower kingdoms' that have inborn *dharma* [nature or Laws of Being]. It is the *dharma* of water to flow. It is the *dharma* of fire to heat or burn. Every expression follows its own instinctive Law of Being, free from the influence of Man's disordered thought. These industrious elements of the lower kingdom can, and do, create a world of harmony, healing and restoring Nature with each cosmic heartbeat.

Man has to learn, understand and, finally, recognise obvious Nature as the Great Mother, who will reveal Her secrets and the inherent *dharma*. Armed with this insight, Man can gain the Supreme Knowledge, the only kind worthy, and be able to rise above shallow intellectualism. Man has to realise that he is the crucible in which transformation of the Cosmic Being is taking place, every second. Through the Yoga of Meditation, Man can enter the fiery heat of personal experience and growth. He gradually learns Nature's ways, one step at a time. The early steps are slow and often painful. The seeker must plough ahead to learn scriptural literature. He must absorb its essence. He will expand intuitively.

Revelation after revelation, Man's inner awareness expands as he opens himself up to personal experiences. Initially, an intellectual understanding of the literature becomes Man's particular understanding. He begins to look at his physical body as the Condensed Cosmic Nutrition of five Bodies and Seven Sheaths. That's when Man realizes that Infinity is not an idea. When he closes his eyes, the darkness he sees is, in fact, Infinity. He is, in all Truth, gazing at – and into – Infinity.

Eventually, Man develops infinite love for God and begins to understand God. The understanding that God is Love and Love is God finally dawns on him. Man begins to seek God all the time, every second of the day, every day of the year. When, and if, Man discovers God in the depth of his meditation, he sees the true vision in his *kutastha,* the third eye, between the two eyebrows [the glabella].

Man, however, starts with the premise that certain things cannot be, that certain effects are just not possible. Most will immediately infer that whatever has been said so far is just not true. I suggest that you be receptive and flexible to new thoughts and ideas. Accepting the Truth, or learning to accept the Truth, is an art that one masters over time.

Instinctively, we search for God outside ourselves – too difficult for those who want to find God over a short period of time. It would take millions of years, thousands of births, deaths and rebirths to reach God through the natural processes of evolution. Raja Yoga is Kriya Yoga – the art of seeking God, to realise that God is 'All' in All. In fact, seeking

God within oneself is the 'fastest' way to find God, for He lives within the field of the divine cave of the brain and *sushumna* [the spinal cord]. It is here that negative and positive polarities of Nature's *gunas* [qualities] exist, as *Tamas* [negative sloth] and *Rajas* [positive qualities of creativity] at opposite poles in the spinal cord.

It is here the fabled Kurukshetra [battlefields] of Life and 'Living' exists, metaphorically speaking. Through the Yoga of Meditation, Man not only discovers these battlefields, but also understands this is where he has to master himself. He can either restrain all outgoing urges by obeying and adhering to Yama [Laws of Ethics], or he can give in to temptation and give in to indulgence. If he gives in to temptation, his *kama* [want] conjures a body preoccupied with his five senses [smell, taste, sight, hearing and touch], his five organs of action [tongue, hands, feet, genitals and anus] and contact with the objects of his want. From the divine cave [the brain and spinal cord], these *nadis* [energy channels] reach out to realise their unmanifest wishes. Kama runs through every fibre, every nerve in the body.

Man has been taught the only way he can be happy, whole and complete is to chase these wants – by his peers, his parents, his teachers. Most of these desires are ingrained in Man's Causal Being, and in this relentless pursuit, he spends his life growing physically, promoting himself emotionally, and maturing intellectually. But when all his wants are supposedly satisfied, Man realises that this happiness is temporary and incomplete. What matters is a 'permanent' state of happiness, but he hasn't been taught how to get there. Is the demand unreasonable? Is happiness Man's birthright?

Only a few know the path to finding happiness. Most are conditioned to wade through the river of human existence, and a fortunate few find a Master to take them across the river... to the other side of human existence. A true Master advises a sincere seeker of spirituality to retrace his steps into himself. He is told, that he has to unshackle himself of the habit of walking outwards, towards objects, emotions and thoughts. To think of the divine cave that exists within him – the space where Man's brain and spinal cord live. Man is then advised to picture the divine cave in others – his family, friends, foes. That's when Man experiences a new understanding, for in the divine cave, there are no friends or foes. In this place, all polarities disappear. The deeper Man goes, the stronger the realisation that everything exists in the divine cave.

Here, in the divine cave, Man finds everything he wants, within himself. Gazing deeply through the inner eye, Man understands the universe flows within him, within his own awareness. The Master then directs a sincere seeker to seek out the spaces between expressions. These spaces seem invisible, because we've been trained to ignore them. Identifying these silent invisibles takes the seeker to an expanse of pure awareness, where everything is filled with an *antardhvani* [vibrating inner sound]. Man, at that point, has reached the substratum of all expression. From then on, the deeper Man delves, the more observant his inner experiences become.

Since the *chakras* [spiritual centres] within the spinal cord vibrate at their own frequency, he hears buzzing, chirping, crackling, running water, tinkling bells and, finally, the roar of the ocean. He may even tread across the rainbow of all the seven colours. Man, however, has come to recognise these as mere appearances along the Journey of Meditation. All along, and after intense perseverance, Man will find God within his being. He will see God in everything. Finally, to him, All will be in God and God will be in All manifestation.

These gains do not, and cannot, crystallise at the first sitting. Man has to learn to energise every part of his body, from the tips of his fingers to the inner precincts of the divine cave. He must learn to harness prana – the life force that exists in his body. He must learn to synchronise and stabilise himself with the rhythm of *prana*. Eventually, Man must learn to transform every atom and cell of his physical body to a state where he experiences no polarities in his own being. Through personal experience, he must come to the conclusion there is no good or bad, no pain or pleasure, no like or dislike.

At that point, and no sooner, the seeker has finally seen the Cosmic Mother, and knows he is part of Her Cosmic Being. His own body has seen a gradual evolution, with the Master Organs in the brain [hypothalamus, pituitary gland] having undergone transformation. These organs trigger responses that cause the release of transformed neurotransmitters and neurohormones that were until now latent. The net effect on the body is a gradual turnover of old cells into new, transformed molecules – rich with new experience and information through personal realisation. The Body, the Mind and the Intellect have been transformed, while Man is now aligned to the Cosmic Mother's Will.

Now, the early purpose of Man seeking God has transcended to Man serving the Cosmic Mother. He has found permanent happiness within himself. He is content spending the rest of his life serving Nature. In his meditative expanse, Man is finally One with both Awareness [Nature] and Consciousness [Spirit].

As opposed to creating a glossary of the Sanskrit terms, I have bracketed their English translations throughout the text, for easier reading. Various explained Figures feature throughout the book, for easier reference to the medical terminology. Of course, the term 'Man' represents humankind in general, and no sexes in particular.

Spirituality is not an easy-to-reach destination, often because of deeply personal and internal struggles. The Mind and Intellect continue to thirst for immortality in a field of constant change – the Mind asks questions that, sometimes, don't have answers. Those fortunate enough to have a Master who lights up the path must cherish the association. For my part, I have used every note and paper of my tutelage to create this text.

Tvameva mata cha pita tvameva Tvameva bandhu cha sakha tvameva Tvameva vidya dravinam tvameva Tvameva sarvam mama deva deva

'You alone are the mother, father, relative and friend. You are the supreme Knowledge and true Wealth. You are my all, oh Lord and Master'.

Dedicated and pledged, with deep gratitude, to my friend, guide, adviser, confidant, my ALL – Swami Chinmayananda – who chiseled me from a rough rock to what I am today... though still imperfect, even after thirty years of study.

Sneh Chakraburtty

Acknowledgements

Swami Tejomayananda and Chinmaya Mission Worldwide, for the use of their voluminous material, written and commented on by Swami Chinmayananda.

The Bhagavad Gita in the Light of Kriya Yoga by Swami Hariharananda of Kriya Yoga Institute.

The Bhagavad Gita by Paramahansa Yogananda of the Self-Realization Fellowship.

Human Physiology by Tony Nader, international president, Maharishi Ayurveda Universities.

B.K.S. Iyengar, author of *Light on Pranayama* and *Light on the Yoga Sutras of Patanjali,* who personally wrote to encourage me and allow me to use parts of his text.

Anil Metre and Vivek Pareek, for their help in the creation of this book.

The Body – Mind – Intellect [BMI] Chart

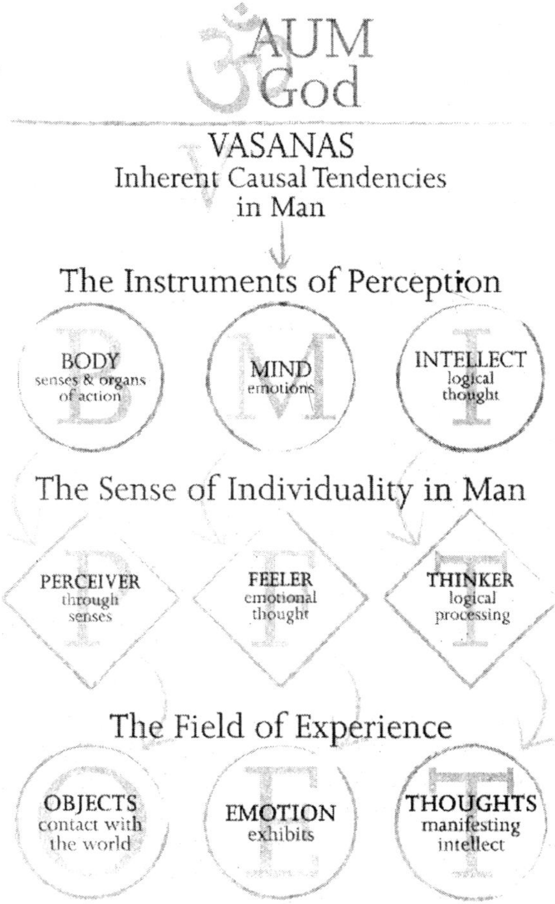

The purpose of the Body-Mind-Intellect [BMI] chart is to align Eastern, popularly called Oriental, and Western or Occidental – thinking. This will help us relate to this text on the same plane, more or less. Every religion on Earth tries to bring about self-transformation in its believers, through self-mastery, so the seeker's life is one of tranquillity, despite outer circumstance. Ancient seekers of the Truth identified that Man experienced the worlds of Objects, Emotions and Thoughts [OET] through the instruments of experience – the Body, Mind and Intellect [BMI].

When identified with the Body and experiencing Objects, Man becomes the Perceiver [P]. Identified with the Mind, Man becomes the Feeler of Emotion [F]. Identified with the Intellect he experiences Thoughts and ideas. Man is now the Thinker [T]. When within the bounds of personality, when Man associates with Objects, Emotions and Thoughts, he is Perceiver-Feeler-Thinker [PFT].

But the truth is... an undistorted experience is neither that of the BMI, nor of the OET.

Then who, exactly, is the PFT? The principle behind Perceiver-Feeler-Thinker [PFT] is the supreme Reality, God or Brahman. The divine substratum, Aum, lends its light and energy to every human being on Earth. Aum is the Holy Spirit, the 'word' of God. Consciousness and Awareness are Spirit and Nature. Combined Spirit and Nature are together Universal Intelligence or Krishna or Christ experienced in the kutastha in meditation. The divine principle or God or Brahman is the Source. Yet He displays through name and form and expresses through the various instruments of the BMI in things, beings and creatures.

Vasanas [V] are inherent urges and habits. They are amassed through many past lives. They influence our minds and therefore actions. They are our unfulfilled, so far unmanifest, desire-motivated tendencies. When they display themselves, they appear as our unique 'Personality'. It is that which drives all our activities in, and towards the world.

Transformation through Meditation

AUM, the Observer, or *Rishi* [vertex] or Spirit *Purusha* with total Knowledge silently watches

Vasanas in silent *Devata* [thalamus] is *Prakriti* [Nature]. She looks at transforming knowledge taking place in the Seed of Man through *sadhana* or willed spiritual practice

Transformed Neurohormones [pituitary gland] and Neurotransmitters [hypothalamus] are released from these Master Glands and influence the BMI especially target endocrine glands

Adjustment of all opinion, feelings and thought takes place, and the quality value of transformation is firmly established on will and effort at meditation. Transformation is visible in the perceptions and actions of Perceiver-Thinker-Feeler [PFT] through Body-Mind-Intellect [BMI]

The alliance with Objects-Emotions-Thoughts [OET] become actions of service to *Prakriti*

Truth lies beyond the instruments of the Body and Mind. To make Truth our own experience, meditation is essential and though the exercise 'involves' the Mind, the experience is beyond the Mind... It is an inner realisation where self meets the Self!

And knowledge of scriptures [available intuitive literature] alone is not enough... There has to be an urgency to imbibe new ideas in the old mind. We need to identify with the pure Self, not the BMI. Countless tries at cutting all identification with the not-Self have to be made. Over time, the seeker's Mind learns to focus during meditation, representing our own limitless nature. Constant practice makes this transformation permanent, as the seeker witnesses a change in the way he uses his BMI. Once this has come about, the seeker becomes a 'witness', aware but not involved. He begins to marvel at this transformation and now sees the worlds of OET from a different perspective. His worldly interactions have a purity, a transformed quality. He begins to see his own self-unfoldment and recognises the unity of the individualistic self with the Cosmic Self.

All the time, the pure self or *rishi,* watches the change, while the causal self or *devata* records the incoming information – through reading, writing, contemplation or meditation – as it is ingrained in the seeker's psyche

Contents

Preface *vii*
Acknowledgements *xiii*
The Body-Mind-Intellect [BMI] Chart *xv*
Transformation through Meditation *xvii*

Section I: Self-Unfoldment and Self-Realisation 1
Blindness to Creation 3
The Secret of Creation: A Mythology 7
Vedanta 13
Sankhyan Philosophy 15
Three Bodies and Five Sheaths 21
The Goal of Life Illumined by a True Master 25
The Tree of Life 27
Body-Mind-Intellect 31
Speech 33
What is the 'Self'? 37
Self-Realisation 39
Yoga 41
Spiritual Paths or The Science of Yoga 43
Kriya Yoga 47
Prana is the Breath of Life 51
Sadhana or Spiritual Effort 55
Raging Conflicts in Spiritual Life 57
Chakras, the Centres of Energy 61
Central Nervous System and Universal Consciousness 67
The Mind as an Organ of the Body 71
Nature Mirrored in the Human Body 77
The Astral Mind in Physiological and Psychological Bodies 79

The Causal Body 85
The Universe Transcribed in the Brain and Spinal Cord 87
Awareness Flows Outwards 89
Expanding Awareness through Spiritual Centres 91
Chitta 95
Knowledge through Intuition 97

Section II: Scientific Evolution 99
Transformation and Evolution of Man and Nature 101
Meditative Inputs and Transformed Outputs 103
Transformation in the Synaptic Spaces of Nerve Tracts 105
Modern Science Recorded in the Ancient Vedas 109
DNA of the Human Cell 113
The Brain and Spinal Cord 115
Feedback Systems of the Brain 121
Sensory Nervous System 121
Sensory and Autonomic Nervous System 122
The 'Looks' of Awareness 125
Action through Motor and Skeletal Systems 127
The Higher Bodily Pacemakers 129
Education 131
Association Nerve Fibres in the Brain Cortex 133
Memory and Automated Reflexes 137
Descending and Ascending Tracts of the Central Nervous System 139
Reaching the Soul through Breath Control 141

Section III: Instincts 145
Automatic Reactions Have Roots 147
Gaining Victory over Thoughts 153
Action and Reaction 157
Maya, the Power of Illusion 159
Spirituality 161
Meditate Constantly 163
Stages in Meditation 165
Spiritual Progress 167
Mind Control 169

Self-Healing 171
Kingdoms of Heaven and of Delusion 173
The Method and Path of a Spiritual Journey 175

Section IV: Scientific Energisation of the Biological Body 177

Yoga 179
Healing Exercises for Transformation 181
Energising Exercises for Transformation 183
Recharging Exercises for Parts of the Body 187
A. To Invoke the Divine Cave 187
B. Relaxing Body Parts into the Divine Cave 188
C. Recharging with Prana from the Divine Cave to Parts of the Body 195
Pranayama 207
Kechri Mudra 209
Maha Mudra 211
The Breath 213
Naad Shravan 217
Jyoti Mudra 219
Raja Yoga is KriyaYoga 221
Changes in the Brain during Concentration 223
Transformation through Natural Living 225
Selfless Action 229
Clearing the Three Nerve Channels 231
Gayatri Mantra 235
Devotion 237

Section V: Spiritual Efforts 239

Sadhana 241
Laws of Prosperity and Success 243
Evolution 245
Remaining Connected 247
Desire, the Seed of Restlessness 249

Foundations of Spiritual Unfoldment 251
Ambitions 253
Ego in the Zone of War 257
Reaching Deathlessness in Meditation 261
Analysing Knowledge 265
Watching the Self 267
Wisdom 269
Harnessing Wisdom 271
Nature and Worship 273
Healing 275
Truth 279
Fire of Knowledge 281
The Past 285
Affirmation 287
Divine Illumination 289

Section VI: Figures 291

Section I

Self-Unfoldment and Self-Realisation

Blindness to Creation

Everything is gifted with Infinite Power, yet Man has no knowledge of how to become one with it. Seeking God is a matter of adhering to Natural Discipline or *dharma,* already inherent in the Laws of Nature. Man must overcome the blindness of his Mind or *avidya,* and combine himself with the power of Wisdom.

Directing life-current decides changing the Mind towards Intuition and, finally, to Wisdom. Awakening the Blind Mind is a return journey along the path of Seven Mystical Centres *[chakras]* found in the brain and spinal cord. Each progressive destination is reached through the perfect mix of effort and 'technique' until every cell of the body is connected with these astral centres. With consistent practice, Man progresses from change to 'changelessness' and, eventually, to God-consciousness.

In fact, this experience through meditation unites – or can unite – not just people, but nations of the world. A rise in the force of these inner currents in individuals, communities, and countries leads – or can lead – to a rise in Total World Intuition and Wisdom. But first, the sense of separation has to be removed from individuals. When individualistic vision sees itself as One with its surroundings, it does not see any difference in, first, the people; then, the nation and, finally, the Universe.

To achieve this state of complete realisation and self-satisfaction is what old masters called perfect happiness, and it is the birthright of every mortal. But before such realisation can exist, one must know what the body is, what it stands for, and where that knowledge can lead. The body is a microcosm within a macrocosm, which is the Universe. In the microcosm, the individual self is the living soul, yet present as the Cosmic Soul in the macrocosm. Using the same analogy, God is the Creator, yet enters Creation as the formless Being.

Although Man's body undergoes constant change as he travels from birth to death, God remains within bodily existence as long as Man keeps Body, Mind and Intellect clean, pure and healthy. It is important to remember that God was in-residence before creation, during creation and will exist eternally, through man's individualistic existence, or through nonexistence, and beyond. In that sense, the human body is designed to find its own Immortality and Infinity. It is said the human body is like an upside–down tree, and the root of the bodily tree is the power of God. The Spirit lives as the ever-witnessing Self, especially at the top of the brain, from where Man watches Man talk, smell, taste, see, hear and touch.

Most of us are unaware and incapable of seeing the roots hidden inside the head, within the cerebral cortex. When the tree is turned upside down, the branches point upwards, towards the roots, or they flow downwards, towards extroverted tendencies of the restive Mind. It is this restlessness of the Mind that separates Man from creation. In reality, there is no separation of spirit from matter. There is, however, a lack of awareness that we are a composite of pure energy and life force and develop at different physical and subtle levels.

Spirituality is about increasing awareness within this symbolic tree. Man must find this tree within himself as it draws a connection with Objects, Emotions and Thoughts [OET]. It is as though each one of us is rooted to the many embedded wants. It is as though we search for us through indulgences. Science asserts the world is perishable and that each mortal is a mixture of Matter and Spirit. The three qualities *[gunas]* of Matter – inertia *[tamas]*, creativity *[rajas]* and harmony *[sattva]* – contribute to the mortal cycle of birth and death. Man fashions his life based on these *gunas* and becomes trapped in his own worldly *karma,* or Law of Cause and Effect.

Wishful thinking and a mechanical routine of prayer and meditation are not enough to transport Man away from this-worldly trap. Though every seeker longs for exactness of information on where and how he can detect God, steady contemplation and knowledge are essential to reach the Higher Realms.

And Man living on a sensory indulgence is like him eating into his own Self. The divisiveness he experiences through the senses – smell, taste and sight – takes him further from the Truth. On the platform of senses, Man senses pain and pleasure, attraction and loathing, light and darkness, hot and cold... only to realise that intermittent pain eventually becomes his permanent suffering.

Life is designed to search for one's own immortality, but the Mind and Intellect are unable to fathom this reality. Preconceived concepts make it more difficult for us to feel God's presence within us because we have different 'concepts' of God, of Infinity. God is about a Collective Vision, and Man's personal vision has to be lofty. Looking at Creation with a downward slant limits one to seeing a world of Objects, Emotions and Thoughts.

The Secret of Creation: A Mythology

A son deceitfully drove a righteous king out of his kingdom. An honest merchant was forced to leave his home by his greedy wife. The king and the merchant met in a forest and exchanged the stories of their misfortunes. They also talked of the love they still have for their families, despite the injustice they had endured, and are surprised to find they still have an attachment to their past lives. Travelling through the forest, they came on a monastery, where a wise old sage invites them to take a break there for as long as they wished. The two stayed and made themselves useful around the monastery. They served the monk and his disciples.

One day, after dinner, the two men engaged the sage in a conversation about 'I', 'Me', and 'Mine'. The forest was chilly and damp, and the sage invited the king and the merchant to join him on a straw mat, close to the fire.

Asked the king, "O sage, why are we still emotionally connected with those who have done us injustice?"

"Your confusion is the result of ingrained tendencies of the restive Mind, which consents to the compelling forces of the three thought-maidens, all daughters of Mother Nature," answered the wise old sage.

The king then asked, "O great sage, what is the intrinsic nature of these thought-maidens and how can we be freed from their coercion and driving force? What is this energy that supports them?"

Began the sage, 'O king, you ask a thousand questions in one sentence. This subject is tied in with the Secret of Creation and cannot be readily revealed to those unfit to suffer this Knowledge. But since you have shown devotion to a monk, I find no cause not to tell you."

He continued, "Before Creation, there was only Truth-Knowledge-Bliss *[sat-chit-anand]*. It was beyond Space. It was Infinite. It heaved a Word and the dazzling Cosmic Mother of Illusion *[Mahamaya]* emerged from It, in the backdrop of the heavenly symphony of the same *Aum* [Amen]."

The king and the merchant listened attentively while the sage shut his eyes, enjoying the story he was about to tell.

"*Mahamaya*, the Cosmic Mother, is the Holy Spirit. She was granted with three daughters, each of whom inherited one of Her three compulsions of Nature. She, the Cosmic Mother, is the first of all Causes. She triggers illusion and delusion *[maya]* by activating Her three qualities *[gunas]*, that are both definable and indefinable. Having identified these qualities, the Cosmic Mother commanded Her daughters to stay in every atom and circumstance She ever created," the sage went on.

The merchant, however, grew impatient, "But who are these three, great sage?"

Replied the sage, smiling patiently, "They are Inertia *[tamas]*, Creativity *[rajas]* and Harmony *[sattva]*. *Mahamaya* is pure Awareness and, thus, also called *Prakriti* [Matter] and is entwined in an embrace with Her male counterpart, Consciousness *[Purusha* or Spirit]."

Continued the sage, "The life-force from *Purusha* urged the energy from *Prakriti* to fill the entire expanse of Nothingness. Radiance from the three daughters filled the void with their innate qualities. With that, *Prakriti* allowed Herself to be as obvious as shades of Darkness or Inertia *[Tamas]*.This beautiful woman's radiant body was black like soot. Inertia's mouth was beautifully shaped. Her eyes were large and kind. In her hands, she carried a garland of empty skulls. She highlighted the need for empty heads while contemplating. The topmost part of the body must be free of ideas. It will allow for successful meditation." The two men intuitively understood the message.

The sage continued, "Having appeared as stylised Darkness, *Tamas* was given tasks she was to perform. 'You will have the ability to measure a spiritual seeker's awareness and remove darkness, hunger, thirst, sleep and want for indulgence' said *Prakriti* [Matter] to Inertia *[Tamas]*, Her first daughter. 'These are also your names and notables of actions you will perform. Those who can discover you through meditating on your names will arrive at happiness,' said *Prakriti.*"

The sage, his throat dry from reciting the tale, turned for a sip of water and then continued, "Having spoken thus, *Prakriti* changed Herself into pure Light and assumed another form that sparkled with the Moon's radiance. This expression, of a fair-skinned woman, held a rosary of letters and a book in her hands. She, too, was given names."

There was a long silence as the sage drifted into his own ecstasy, communicating with the divine powers and grace of *Prakriti's* second daughter.

"And what are these names?" interrupted the merchant.

The sage awakened to the present with a smile. He had enjoyed that brief interlude with Creativity *[Rajas].*

"*Prakriti* said to Her second daughter, 'You are *Rajas* [Creativity]. You will be known as Supreme, Pervasive Knowledge, Wisdom, Creative Energy, Mother of the Mind and Fulfiller of Wishes," began the sage. He continued, "The Cosmic Mother then commanded both *Tamas* and *Rajas* to bring into being a male. 'The male must equate with her innate natures.' The Mother then transformed Herself into Harmony *[Sattva]*, the third daughter."

"What was special about Harmony *[Sattva]*, O Sage?" asked the king, absorbing the sage's words.

"Harmony was seated on the Golden Womb. It held the wants of every plant, bird, beast and man in the previous period of Dissolution of Creation, or *pralaya,"* answered the sage. He added, "The Mother then told *Sattva* she is Prosperity and True Wealth. Man arrives here through meditation," said the sage.

The sage went on, "Inertia *[Tamas]* apprised her male half. He mirrored Peaceful Energy *[Shiva]*. She asked the Cosmic Mother *[Mahamaya* or *Prakriti]* to earmark his utilitarian qualifications. 'He will be known as Reliever of Suffering, Melody, Fulfiller of Desires, and Peace,' said the Mother.

"Creativity *[Rajas]*, the second daughter, turned to her male counterpart, Vishnu, and asked the Cosmic Mother for his bonds to Creation. 'He will be known as Pervading Consciousness, the Real Organiser and Sustainer of all Creation, Ruler of the Senses and Lord of True Wealth. He will destroy thoughts. He will spread the Energy of Infinite Goodness,' said Prakriti."

"Harmony *[Sattva]* then asked the Mother to define the characteristics of her male half, *Brahma.* Having told her he would be known as the Creator, she said Brahma is the 'Knower' of Consciousness. This Self is known by the self through systematic worship," said the sage.

It was well into the night, and the mellifluous sounds of the forest engulfed them. There was a long silence, until, finally, the merchant asked, "What is the purpose of these transformations, O learned one?"

"This can only be understood through the eyes of Wisdom gained through the fire of meditation, as a personal experience," answered the sage, "The uninitiated may not understand, or may not be willing to, the meaning of this secret... That She is the repository of He."

"She, who is Awareness *[Prakriti]*? The idea that She and Consciousness *[Purusha]* are One?" probed the king.

The sage nodded, smiling.

"What happened then?" asked the merchant, relishing

the story, and wanting to know more.

The sage resumed his story, "Peace *[Vishnu]* and Creativity *[Rajas]* invited Harmony *[Sattva]* and the Creator *[Brahma]* to crack the Golden Egg *[hiranyagarbha]*."

Anticipating the question, the sage continued. "Within this egg lie the primary essences of products of Creation. The capacities of five Elements [space, air, fire, water and earth] are embedded here. Memories of past existence of both movable and immovable forms are there. Information on what is yet to come is not forgotten. Rajas and Vishnu immediately initiated protection and nourishment of Creation for the next appointed Cycle."

"How long does the Cycle of Creation normally last?" asked the merchant.

"It undergoes four stages of human evolution, once every million years," replied the sage. He then added with a twinkle, "But this would make a new story by itself."

After a short pause, the sage returned to the subject of the three daughters and Creation. He consolidated the discussion with a conclusion. "At the appointed time, Inertia *[Tamas]* and Peaceful Energy *[Shiva]* will bring about the Dissolution of Creation in a Deluge *[pralaya]*." With that, the sage stood up to retire to his chambers.

The king and the merchant looked following the sage as he walked away. They realised they must interpret the Story of Creation by themselves. To decipher the duress of the Cosmic Mother and Her tendencies in plant, creature and human being required scriptural knowledge. Contemplation and concentration is the insinuated path. The sage teacher had spoken.

After what seemed exhausting hours, the two retired for the night. They concluded they have inherited tendencies from the three daughters. To transcend these innate tendencies, they must learn to transcend restlessness of the Mind.

The next morning, they beseeched the sage to teach them the scientific technique of contemplation. The sage, sensing the earnestness of their request, agreed. And after seven years of sincere meditation, the king and the merchant had learned how to transcend Nature's three compulsions: Inertia, Creativity and Harmony.

Is there a moralistic message to this story? Learn to believe, with faith in a teacher. Learn to understand, what is read, heard and thought. Learn to contemplate with sincerity.

Vedanta

Vedanta is the Philosophy of Eastern thought. It upholds the doctrine of Pure Nondualism. I am the Self is conditional nondualism because God and I are One. Historically, this philosophy has proved to be the most enduring. It is also the oldest and most widely developed philosophy in over six thousand years.

It was developed by philosophers of the past and confirmed by sages who came after them. They are mystics who live in caves similar to those of the Himalayas. From these stratospheres they continue to guide civilisation through meeting and understanding. Uninterrupted and unbroken investigation has led the learned people or yogis, to gather discoveries about Truth, Values of Life and The Art of Living. Philosophers continue to realise Man depends on their grace. The world, which we live in, wants their protection. New ideas or thoughts, produced through their critical examination, are not suppressed. The questions are answered, and the original is continuously expanded and enlarged. In fact, these men of wisdom are the stewards of the planet, and have protected it from harm for aeons.

The result is that *Vedanta* grows and matures with the centuries and provides the widest cultural base of Indian philosophy, religion and ethic. It provides India with an enduring culture, because it lays down the foundation of 'civilisation' and recognises the common values of all religions.

The *Sanskrit* term for philosophy is *darshana.* It means 'world-view'. Its aim is a comprehensive understanding of the objective world. The roles of rational consciousness, goodness, beauty and their crowning reality are studied.

Vedanta belongs to one of the six orthodox schools of Indian Philosophy. It is the heart of *Sankhyan darshana* – *a* world-view through reasoning.

Sankhyan philosophy uses reason, analysis and reflection to comprehensively survey Nature. Its founder is *Kapila,* the sage born in Pushchair, Nepal, over five thousand years ago. *Sankhyans* insist that *Prakriti* [Matter] is not substance but energy. It has the astronomical potential for creative evolution. They accept the Law of Qualities. The three qualities [gunas] of energy are specific. Sattva or Harmony has the features of knowledge, goodness and brightness. Rajas or Creativity is dynamism, and surges with movement. If it arouses uncontrolled, it leads to sorrow. Tamas or Inertia tends towards monotony. These three gunas control the direction of evolution in all things on Earth. *Sankhyans* also accept the Law of Causality, of cause and effect. Cause is the potential power and seed for fulfillment of the future.

Sankhyans insist that Man is a product of his past. His past births determine his present. The present foretells his future. They grant the Law of Duality or Relativity [likes and dislikes], fixes the character fabric of the person in his present expression. They also say the health of the Body must be cared for. It is the gateway to self-realisation. But attachment to the body and its demands is discouraged. Lessons in Soul Culture are received through a teacher. Man is encouraged to attach himself to the indwelling Spirit with every breath.

Sankhyan Philosophy

Sage Kapila offered mankind the *Sankhyan* philosophy. It is also a *Vedic* philosophy, penned and saved for posterity in black and white, over five thousand years ago. He perpetuated and proved that Consciousness and Awareness are our real nature. He said evolution is fulfilled when we discover these states. *Vedanta* pointed to the reflective writings at the end of the *Vedas*. They repeatedly affirm this world of sense objects is not genuine. This also happens to be a *Buddhist* view. It is only a venerable emergence that retreats with legitimate Knowledge. Its reality ends with understanding. Fulfilling its break-up is like an undeniable ghost to a fearful man. The 'reality' of a mirage also disappears as one approaches it.

The Eternal alone Is.

The world and individualistic egocentric ideas are a fantasy. The sense of a separate existence is a superimposition on Truth. Because self-inquiry is the human mind's eternal search, Man always asks the same questions. What engulfs everything everywhere? Where does all this repose?

The answers to this timeless inquisitiveness are universal. They are found in the words of sages of all times and climes. *Kapila* discovered the Absolute within himself. He knew the answers to Man's questions. He knew the answers are not in the relentless search of the outward world. Only by retracing steps from the outside to the inner world can Man find himself. Man has to enter his own self first. *Yogis* before him had done that, he said. They identified the origin of the material world from within. After all, the material world, like everything else, dissolves into the same Absolute *Brahman* or God.

Brahman or God before expression Is.

He is Existence-Knowledge-Bliss or *Sat-Chit-Anand.* It is the Supreme Source, the Infinite. Like the Sun or Spirit that becomes distinctly striking through its rays as Matter, He chooses the fashion of exposition for His own pleasure. He displays Himself as many names and forms in many appearances. The Unmanifest decides on becoming the Manifest.

Purusha or Spirit is brought into existence as male. He stands in magnificent isolation, free of want, emotion and activity. As the everlasting Observer, He is a perfect example of spiritual entropy. He is the Unmanifest Universal Psychic Principle that permeates and witnesses Nature. Yet He stands at a distance, uninvolved and immutable. It is *Purusha* who breathes life into Matter and enlivens it with His stimulus.

Prakriti or Matter is the Universal Physical Principle. She controls the power of *maya* or illusion and delusion. *Maya* is integral to the Law of Qualities of Matter or *gunas.* She governs the Law of Cause and Effect or *karma* and the Law of Relativity or Dualism [likes and dislikes, or *raaga-dvesha*]. *Prakriti* is created as female, dancing in action, thought and feeling. It is *Prakriti* who unfolds into multiplicity of this cradle of humanity and materialisation.

On a stirring backdrop of *Aum, Purusha* invests in *Prakriti* the power to perform the Dance of Creation in each *kalpa* or Cycle of Creation. Through every quarter of this cycle of one million years She alters the blueprint of Her Dance of Design of the Universe. She moves from an unmanifest platform to manifestation.

She weaves a panoramic Creation. At first She dances in front of him, and then away from Him. Her stunning magic of order, logic, beauty and love are transcribed in visible creation. From within Her body, *Prakriti* unloads the essence of the five gross elements [earth, water, fire, air and space]. She lends Herself to creating their sensory counterparts. The five subtle senses are smell, taste, sight, sound and touch.

They come under the jurisdiction of the Mind. With *Purusha's* help She enlivens the energy in elements. All senses with physiological roles [respiration, digestion, excretion, circulation and intellection] become active. Enlivening happens by breathing in life force or *prana. Prana* allows the organs of action [tongue, hands, feet, genitals and anus] to work.

By means of the cosmic ego, intellect and mind, this personality is made. She lends it the Awareness of *Prakriti.* In this manner the Cosmic Mother, gives birth to the twenty-four natural building blocks in birds and creatures, and caters to all their needs. Although seemingly interdependent, She becomes separate bits of individual awareness, in feelings and mood.

Individualised mind-intellect-ego or *chitta* is an independent personality. It is the microcosmic counterpart of the macrocosmic Cosmic Intellect *[Mahat],* who works for the Cosmic Whole. The twenty-four matter elements of *Prakriti* joined with *Purusha* become the twenty-five units that make up the human body.

Mahat is the unevolved primary cell of Nature. From it came the material world. It is like the microprocessor of a computer. Inventories of every desire *[kama],* action *[karma],* likes and dislikes *[raaga-dvesha],* tendency *[vasana]* and quality of actions *[gunas]* are embedded within this seed. Also embedded in the primary cell are the twenty-four basic formational elements *[tattvas].* It allows unmanifest wants to be perpetuated into the obvious world.

The design of each of these twenty-four constructional elements or *tattvas* exists, in essence, in Matter or *Prakriti's* Causal Being. Here they exist as a permanent record of all cause and effect:

- The five gross elements or *pancha-maha-bhutas,* that is, earth, water, fire, air, space.
- The five sense perceptions or *pancha-tan-matras,* using the five sense organs *gyana-indriyas*

experience smell [by the eyes], taste [with the tongue], sight [the eyes], hear [the ears] and touch [the skin].

- The five physiological life forces or *prana* are also sometimes referred to as the vital airs. These are – *pranaya* for respiration. *Apanaya* is for excretion. *Vyanaya* is for circulation. *Samanaya* is for assimilation. And *udanaya* is for intellection.
- There are also five organs of action or *karmaindriya.* For speech or *vaak* the tongue is put to use. Working hands work through *paani* and working legs function through *paada. Upastha* is for sexual activity and *payu* is for excretion.
- The ego is *ahamkar* and the mind is *manas.* The intellect is *buddhi* and the self-personality becomes obvious as ego, thought and restlessness, also called *chitta.*

Creation takes place with Spirit or *Purusha* breathing life as *prana* into Matter. This is the breath of God that supports the Universe. This breath constantly echoes as a melodious symphonic Aum, Hum, or Amen. The constructional units of creation are supported by It and exist because of It. Existence, therefore, grows and changes around *Purusha* and *Prakriti.*

The Mind *[manas]* acts as the bridge between the physical body and the individualised soul [self]. This sensory mind is subtle. As 'Me', the self-fulfills its ambitions and agrees to its pleasures through the mind, which acts as a mirror. The body serves as an instrument of enjoyment and attainment. Because the self [Me] is vaguely aware of the soul [I], he intuitively knows mortal birth has a purpose. He must use the twenty-four constructional units of the body to separate the self from the Self. He knows he must discover the identity of the soul.

In every creation, the Creator embeds Himself as the Soul *[so]* in the body *[ham].* Man does not need external means to Self-realisation. God pervades him, as He does everything else. Man's search for God is like ice searching for water. Man is a microcosmic expression of macrocosmic Matter or *Prakriti*. Pervading it in every atom of matter is the indwelling energy of the Spirit or *Purusha*.

Everything that's visible is comprised of eight ingredients: earth, water, fire, air, space, mind, intellect, and ego. These are the faculties of Nature. They rule through five lower spiritual centres in the spinal cord and two in the brain. The mind, intellect and ego are, together, the personality of an unevolved *chitta*. It is their innate inclination to make Man extroverted and materialistic.

The five tendencies, ambitious want, anger, greed, attachment and pride, display their temperament in the first five untamed energy plexuses or *chakras*. Jealousy and ego stay in the unharnessed sixth, or *ajna chakra*, in the medulla. In its pure form it reflects in the *kutastha*, above the pituitary. The lower centres *[chakras]* are the seats of delusion or *maya*. They reflect the materialistic attractions through Nature's illusory forces. To rise to the upper *chakras*, one must practise the scientific technique of meditation – *Raja* or *Kriya Yoga* – as taught by a realised Master.

Three Bodies and Five Sheaths

God is One. He is the Impersonal Soul, *Brahman*. He displays Himself as the other half – the Universe or the Cosmic Mother. He enters every atom, every cell, and becomes the all-pervading spirit of Existence, inherent Knowledge and Bliss, or *sat-chit-anand.*

The Soul created two forces. The centrifugal force makes Man an extrovert. The centripetal force makes Man an introvert. Man, however, ends extroverted as if required by Nature. His attention is drawn to money, food and sex. Under the sway of Mother Nature's intrinsic *maya,* Man thinks himself as a separate fragmented entity. He is convinced he is detached from God. However, a spiritual journey within leads Man to linger over this misconception. It forces him to come face-to-face with the silent witness of the three states of his being – waking, dreaming and sleeping. Man now realises he is an embodied soul. He needs to analyse his own 'expression' to discover the real Truth.

According to *Vedanta,* three frames of body *[sharira]* envelop the soul:

- GROSS *[sthula sharira]* frame: the anatomic body
- SUBTLE *[sukshma sharira]* frame: the physiological, psychological, intellectual body
- CAUSAL *[karana sharira]* frame: the ideational body

The three bodies are themselves made up of five inter-penetrating and inter-dependent sheaths *[koshas]*.

The gross body *[sthula sharira],* the anatomical sheath of physical atoms, is born of physical food and nourishment. It is called *annamaya kosha* or the gross food sheath.

The subtle body or *sukshma sharira* is made up of three interpenetrating sheaths. They are the physiological sheaths or *pranamaya kosha,* the psychological sheath or *manomaya kosha* and the intellectual sheath or *gyanamaya kosha.* Breath through *prana* is the subtle life force that enlivens these sheaths with rejuvenation of energy. The physiological sheath or *pranamaya kosha* includes the respiratory *[pranaya],* circulatory *[vyanaya],* excretory *[apanaya],* digestive and assimilative *[samanaya]* and nervous *[udanaya]* systems.

The psychological sheath or *manomaya kosha* transforms awareness with feelings and sense-desiring motivations. It does not depend on any subjective judgment.

The intellectual sheath or *gyanamaya kosha* affects the intellectual processes of reasoning and judgement. It is gathered from subjective encountering, both past and present.

The causal body or *karana sharira* is the subtlest of the three bodies. It is an ideational sheath of joy *[anandamaya kosha].* It is composed of the essence of twenty-four units of the gross and subtle bodies. It has on record all the informational data recorded in Man, in the course of his many lives. The experience of awakening after a refreshing sleep describes this structure. Total absorption of the seeker in meditation is an indirect reference to the meeting in *anandamaya kosha.*

The skin encloses all *shariras* [bodies] and *koshas* [sheaths]. They are at and from different levels, mingled with the individualised self. The twenty-four elements can't do anything without the Soul remaining within. The soul stays in the thalamus or *kutastha.* It breathes through the medulla, the instrumentality and the 'mouth' of God. The medulla engages the body in *prana.* It also gives Man the authority to make out the Spirit. That's why we have a Living Body.

Through meditation, Man can withdraw from the five lower senses. It reaches the Soul centre in the *kutastha* behind and between the two eyebrows. In the depths of meditation, Man meets two other sheaths. *Chittamaya kosha* or the changed, combined mind-intellect-ego complex in the thalamus, which is intimately connected to Awareness of *Prakriti*. And there is *Chitmaya kosha,* the sheath of Consciousness or *Purusha*. It is found in the fontanel above the thalamus, but between the vertex and the pineal gland.

The last two sheaths, *Chittamaya kosha* and *Chitmaya kosha,* are realms of superconsciousness. Here all sense of the body and worldliness disappears. Unless Man realises his body is a temple of God, he can't know that God stays within. When St. Teresa of Avila described these seven sheaths, she spoke of them as the 'seven veils'. To reach the Core of one's being, one needs to shed every one of these veils or sheaths. And for this, one needs an experienced teacher or *guru*.

The Goal of Life Illumined by a True Master

Moksha is Liberation. It is the goal of Life. To arrive at Self-realisation is to fulfil Life's purpose. From facing the Soul within, immortality approaches forward. At that point, the self or individuality ceases to be. Wants that lead to imperfect happiness disappear. The Mind coalesces into a 'desireless' state of perfect happiness, satisfaction, peace and security.

A preceptor is indispensable on the spiritual journey. He creates a need for liberation in the disciple. A *guru* makes Subtle God *[gu]*, Perceptible *[ru]*. A real *guru* takes the disciple from darkness to light. This is possible because he is himself Self-realised. Before the disciple comes on a preceptor, he is preoccupied with extroverted activities of his self. He is lost in the forest of bodily bondage and worldly pleasure. A preceptor awakens a disciple to the fact that he is the Self. He reveals to him the path.

The spiritual truths that have been offered to seekers for centuries are not products of speculation. They are ideals that have been realised and repeatedly confirmed by spiritual Masters. Personal experiences in the depth of meditation or practice of *yoga* are the means. Through complete withdrawal from the external world, sages have, over centuries, explored the inner world of *sat-chit-anand* or Existence-Knowledge-Bliss. *Yoga is* not acrobatics or just a stay-fit *mantra,* it is union of Man with God.

Though many teachers may come and go during a seeker's life, there can be only one *guru*. The relationship between a *guru* and his disciple is eternal. Only the pure, sincere heart of a seeker is capable of attracting a *guru*. Many stories highlight the importance and critical need of a guru to illumine the path to Self-realisation. Adi Shankara did just that. This *yogi* lived over two thousand years ago. He described the hallmarks of a true *guru:*

"He is well versed in the Vedas [Holy Scriptures]. He is sinless, unaffected by want and best among the knowers of Brahman. He has withdrawn himself into Brahman. He is calm. He is like a fire that has consumed its fuel. He is a boundless reservoir of mercy."

To seekers and preceptors, Adi Shankara further described the goal of Life and why the need for a *guru:*

"There are three things that are, indeed, rare. They are arrived at only by the grace of God. These are a human birth, the desire for liberation and the protecting care of a perfect sage."

The Tree of Life

The Human Nervous System resembles an upside-down or upturned *peepal* or *ashwatha* tree [Ficus religious]. The brain and its six sets of nerve rootlets are on top, and the spinal cord is below. This is the tree of life. It must be entered through meditation. By entering the root of the tree of life in the brain, Man can move beyond his individuality. Through self-unfoldment and eventual self-realisation that he is, and always was the soul, he draws nearer to the aim of existence as Man.

The brain is lodged in the skull, the dwelling place of the Soul. The spinal cord, starting at the base of the skull extends to the upper lumbar region, posterior to the umbilicus. It is made up of specialised nerve cells and fibres bundled together within the vertebral column. From the cord distal to the lumbar area of the abdomen, thick nerve bundles descend towards the tailbone or coccyx, as the cauda equina. All these nerves are nerve channels or *nadis* that shift life force or *prana* to and from the various body parts.

Meditative exercises are taught to strengthen the brain and spinal cord. Experienced teachers produce adjustments. Exercises persuade candidates of *yoga* to begin physical and mental regeneration and rejuvenation.

But one fact remains. Man *did* take birth to satisfy his unfulfilled wants. He will and must fulfil these in accordance with the Laws of Nature. While on this part of his life's journey, Man often becomes a slave to desires. By leading a life of turbulence to satisfy his needs of wealth, sex, food, alcohol and so forth, he forgets the object of human birth. He forgets it is liberation through self-discipline. For centuries, Man has been taught to first fulfil the four goals in life. They must be fulfilled under laws of virtue:

- Man should live a life of morality or *dharma.* Without ethical discipline, spiritual attainment or liberation is impossible.
- Man should gain wealth or *artha* only through righteous means. Wealth itself is meant for independence and the higher pursuits in life. It is not intended for lasting materialistic joy.
- Man should satisfy all his ambitions and passions or *kama* in moderation, without harming his body.
- Man must learn to transcend his senses to be freed or for *moksha.*

Only an enlightened Man can understand that power, pleasure, wealth and knowledge pass away. They don't amount to freedom. He, therefore, must rise above the pituitary above the eyebrows and enter a higher realm. Here Nature's tendencies don't disturb his journey towards self-realisation.

In the *Bhagavad Gita,* Krishna revealed His secret address within the divine cave of the brain and spinal cord. Awareness of everything that happened in the past, the present and that which will happen in the future is condensed in the human body, said Krishna. A restricted description of the human form is incomplete. It must include a description of God. Then it includes everything - the Whole.

Man's body is a materialization of God's Thought. It is condensed Awareness-Consciousness. Once Man is convinced of this, he realises his own immortality. He is now capable of the highest devotion. He gains entry into the journey by concentrating on every part of his own body *[ham].* He walks until he enters the divine cave. Man watches Life as breath *[prana].* He enters the divine cave with each inspiration. He experiences for himself this breath enlivens every part of his body *[ham].* He finally witnesses the silence or Soul *[so]* within.

There is no need to question God any more. His personal experience of *sa* is beyond all explanation. He needn't waste his intellect in thought.

Body-Mind-Intellect

The body is the home of *Brahman* or the Infinite. Since the Body-Mind-Intellect play a vital role in arriving at the fourfold aims of life, Man must keep his body in a healthy and competent condition. Well-being is a precarious balance of the body, mind and spirit. The body and mind come together in *yoga* of meditation only if this balance is achieved.

To practice meditation, one must have a healthy physical body, free of the aches and pains of living. Most of us, however, don't have the expertise to care for the body and its exposures... in effect, the damage is done. One has to energise one's body and the tools for this are exercises taught in *Raja yog*. With the help of the enlivening *prana*, the power of will calls upon bodily energy, to heal and bring every abused physical cell back to health.

The interrelationship of Body-Mind-Intellect is essential. It is based on cooperation. An elegant relationship of *Prakriti* or Matter with *Purusha* or Spirit is made possible and is necessary. The synthesis of *Prakriti* and *Purusha* leads to freedom.

The Vibrating Energy in *Prakriti* connected with life-force *Prana* is the 'mains' into which every form is plugged. The 'cables' of connection is the incoming breath. *Prana* is the substratum and life force that nurtures every atom in the visible Universe and beyond. Sexual energy is the most basic outward expression of life force, which crystallises as '*ojas*'. This is perfected essence of healthy bodily tissues. *Ojas* is hugely powerful and should be respected. It finds expression in the warmth of our emotions, the passion of our intellect and fires our idealism.

Our physical essence is the egg -of sperm-ovum. Similarly, our spiritual essence is the individualised self. It displays as activity of mind and the brilliance of our intellect as *tejas.* Renunciation of indulgence for pleasure is a step towards disengagement. It should not be thought of as a sterile rejection. There is a moral aspect to all of Man's activities, including sexual behaviour. It is the offensive and immoral use of this potent energy that is rejected in spiritual exercises.

Prakriti, to the traditional *Vedic* mind, is the personification of abstract spiritual truth. As *deva* the Holy Spirit is the female consort of *Purusha,* God the Son. He is also referred to as *Rishi* in the 'Transformation through Meditation' chart. *Purusha* and *Prakriti* together communicate as Universal Intelligence of the Infinite or *Brahman* while enduring in the Christ or Krishna Centre.

The individualistic self, 'Me', is the intellectualized ego. It is an adulterated state of the normal blameless matchless *Prakriti.* Mired in the delusion and illusion of *Maya* and encouraged by the visible world's physical properties or *gunas,* Man begins to believe he is the physical being. The unenlightened ego doesn't know that distorted *chitta* and Consciousness *[chit]* enliven the inert physical body we worship so dearly.

Speech

The Tongue is the most powerful organ of the body. The body is not made 'to live by bread alone, but by every word that advances out of the mouth of God'. [Matthew 4:4 & Luke 4:4]. Only thorough control over the tongue, even while it speaks, can Man be allowed to taste the Truth. This is because the tongue has the ability to express spiritual truth.

The practice of *Raja Yoga* allows one to have complete control over all parts and organs of one's body. One learns to avoid anger, hypocrisy, pride and cruelty. Speech that is kind is aimed at bettering humankind. Through speech came the first utterance of God.

Creation, according to tradition, began with a Word. That word was *AUM* (*amen, amin, hum*). The beginning of every form of Speech is the Holy Spirit. She is *Prakriti* or *Shakti, Mahamaya* or the Cosmic Mother. *Vedic* thought has recognised and outlined four levels of speech:

- AUDIBLE SPEECH is spoken from the throat when Man is awake. This is literal or coarse speech. It is a reaction to some form of stimulation.
- THINKING SPEECH is spoken from the heart. It is obvious as pure thought. It is experienced in dreams. This happens after 'thinking deeply' about something.
- ILLUMINED SPEECH is spoken as a 'gut feeling'. It originates from the navel. It reveals in its purity in deep sleep. In meditation, it reveals itself as views of the 'Illumined Word'. It occurs as announcement. It is a sign of the Holy Spirit's grace.

- TRANSCENDENT SPEECH cannot be put into words. It is 'felt' in divine words of silence. It is a pure consciousness and realisation: *Tat Tvam Asi* [That You Are] and *Aham Brahma Asmi* [I am All That] are examples of spoken silence.

The power of speech must be understood from its root. The energy of its awareness must be allowed to fulfil its highest potential through meditation. The power of speech and the restless breath must be tamed by drawing them inwards with *mantras.* This allows speech to originate from the root centre of the subtle body. The spiritual centres *[chakras]* in the navel, the heart and the throat must all be conquered by Man. Only then will it allow speech to enter the fourth level of illumined perception.

Meditation is a progressive learning. It aims at allowing us to reach the silent consciousness, the 'I', the Soul. The first stage involves harnessing both *tamas* [inertia] and *rajas* [restlessness]. Once complete equilibrium is reached *Sattva* or harmony is achieved. This physical-entropy is necessary to arrive at the higher goal of spiritual-entropy. In the unearthing of 'I' meditation is the *yoga* that connects the unfolding self with the Soul. It is a spiritual movement that allows Man to reach heavenly stillness and silence.

Speech has two aspects. *Inaudible* or intuitive speech is the language of the heart. This is not a mere chattering in the mind. And the *audible* speech which, when cultivated and refined, becomes intuitive. Its objective is to relay the power of the mind, to gain insight for a collective good.

Speech is a form of energy or *Shakti.* It is present in every one of the centres or *chakras.* The melody is of the *pranava* or Cosmic Sound. It is also referred to as the Comforter or the Holy Spirit in the Bible. The Power of Speech is connected to the Spirit. If divorced from emotion and mental activity, it can lift Man to the highest platform of being, through its creative energy. Control over speech is the most important part of self-development. It develops as the practitioner advances through self-effort or *sadhana*. There are three stages to unfolding speech:

- There is a correction of mind-emotion DESIRE, based on a philosophy of its purity.
- The mind achieves an aesthetic energy and WILLS an action for a particular improvement.
- The will to improve is EMPOWERED by awareness of *Aum*. This persuades speech to become a Power for the individual, as well as, for collective consciousness.

Speech that empowers one's life force should be attached with Will to create words in the service of others, for collective good. If the mind is a collection of thoughts and if thoughts crystallise to become speech, then mind-power can be heightened. Such achievements happen with the use of a single potent word or *mantra* in focused meditation. This intense self-effort or *sadhana* is for mind control. It activates and expands the latent Cosmic Forces within each one of us.

Coarse or literal speech is audible. It is obvious at the level of conventional human words or language. Such audible speech originates in the throat. It is connected to our senses in our waking state.

When thinking deeply, we begin to ponder. Speech earns a creative force of beauty. It takes on a dream-like state of thoughts. It originates from emotions of the heart.

When speech picks up the power of illumination and perception, it does so because of universal truths. This veracity underlines all events and all things. These are obvious in deep sleep as the essence of thought. Man senses it in the gut at the navel.

When speech becomes a revelation of the forces behind all Creation, it is the experience of a happening, a realisation. This is transcendental speech of the super conscious state.

Her thoughts and words cease to be. And there is only the silent vibration of *Aum.*

In the beginning of any spiritual journey, the power of speech must be studied from the first *chakra,* the coccygeal plexus. With progress, the seeker allows the enlivening energy of Awareness to move up gradually. Restraint and adherence to speech-control allows the seeker to rise to his higher potentials. He begins to hear the inner sound, emanating from the divine cave both in the brain and spinal cord.

The music of this inner sound allows the seeker to listen and witness breath. Over time, the sound of an inner *mantra* combines with *prana.* It takes the seeker to different levels of the seven *chakras* of the divine cave. The brain and spinal cord is magnetised. Speech will, then, gradually harmonise itself with the Divine Cosmic World.

But first, there's the issue of refining audible speech, which is where the seeker starts. Our tendencies may be coarse, but sincere effort can correct all reflective responses ingrained in our causal being.

What is the 'Self'?

The self-unfolded is the Self-realised. The self is 'Me' the individualised and Self is the Soul *[purusha]*, the 'I' of Mankind. It is the spiritual treasure that cannot be found anywhere, except inside one's self. It is our innermost deity. It is hidden in every being as an all-pervasive light of Existence, Knowledge and Bliss. To discover the Self [Sa], one must penetrate the veils of individual Nature *[Ham]*, layer after layer.

The total Self can be realised in the *kutastha.* This is the sixth *chakra* [medullary centre] that is reflected from the *ajna* to the visual cortex of the brain in the occiput. This reflection then remains in the thalamus above the pituitary, behind the glabella in the *kutastha* between the two eyebrows. Many have called it the third eye. Others have imagined it vaguely as a centre of Awareness. It can be experienced and realised as pure awareness through the scientific technique of *Raja* or *Kriya Yoga.* The individualistic self, when self-unfolded, is a changed *chitta.* Meditation allows the chitta-personality of mind-intellect-ego to metamorphose from 'Me' to 'I', the only enduring Reality. Here my continuous experience is that 'I am'. This feeling of 'I am' is beyond all objects, emotions, or thoughts [OET]. I know 'I am' not my body, mind or intellect [BMI]. I realise 'I am' not the performer, feeler or thinker [PFT].

Through the body, Man is the 'perceiver'. Through the mind, he is the 'feeler'. And through the intellect, he is the 'thinker' [PFT]. The PFT looking at objects, emotions, and thought is a *bhoga,* or a mere mortal enjoying the world. But I am in truth the unenlightened personality or *chitta.* And I also know that 'I am' more than the ordinary PFT. Turned inwards, I am the *yogi* or spiritual seeker. I am on the path to decoding the individualistic self while an unenlightened awareness *chitta*. 'I am' on a journey towards self-unfoldment to meet the Soul who is the enlightened *chitta*. When my Awareness is purified through self-realisation, I will enter the hall of Consciousness or *chit*. Here I will finally merge with *Sat-Chit-Anand* [Existence-Knowledge-Bliss]. That is supreme Self-realisation.

Seekers have often asked this question: If *Prakriti* acts under the direction of *Purusha,* how is it possible for *Prakriti* to hide *Purusha?* Well, just as the sun can evaporate water and yet remain hidden in the mist, so too can *Prakriti* cover the Spirit with body consciousness.

In fact, *Prakriti* covers the Self with three types of veils. They all are obstacles to meditation. The qualities or *gunas [tamas-rajas-sattva]* of Nature exist in every human body. A particular quality may predominate, depending on which of the three astral nerve channels are used for breathing. If breath flows mainly through the left parasympathetic astral channel *[ida]* sloth *[tamas]* is the characteristic. If breath flows mostly through the right sympathetic nerve channel, *rajas* predominate and the person is restless, energetic and materialistic. If breath flows through both channels equally it does so through the central spinal cord *[sushumna]*. The person is content *[sattva]*, is attached to knowledge and leads a simple lifestyle.

Although innate in the physical body, all qualities *[gunas]* reach Man from food. It is diet that gives Man energy and vitality of *rajas* or makes him idle and slothful as *tamas*. People attached to materialism find it difficult to transcend the *gunas*. If people try to stay rooted in truth, they can achieve all-round development by learning the science of breath. They learn to remain cautious with every breath. To watch the Self drawing *prana* towards the *kutastha,* with each inspirational breath, is to be constantly aware. Gradually, they make out the *Sa* or Self in every activity of the body. Purified by such continuous awareness, they don't allow passion, anger, greed, hypocrisy or pride to disturb their awareness.

Self-Realisation

Man cannot make spiritual progress simply by suppressing worldly activities and fighting idleness. Spiritual evolution is not repression. It is sublimation of lower tendencies for a higher purpose. Regulating life needs the touch of a realised Master. He or she must be well versed in the science of breath control. Breath control, in effect, brings about mind control. In a meditative state, life begins to regulate itself in tandem with changes in breath. Consistent and endless effort at breath control brings about transformation. The seeker is then able to give up temptation, restlessness and attachment to materialism.

One achieves self-realisation when one relentlessly follows the path of *yoga* or union with the ideal goal of Life, the Spirit. The *Sutras* [aphorisms] in old *Vedic* scriptures are instructions one must understand to define and experience God. This study needs a silent and alert mind. Vigilance is necessary to prevent the seeker of spirituality from falling back to familiar, habituated ways.

If the body and mind refuse to cooperate, the seeker must begin to train under a preceptor. Once the conflict within him or her is resolved, the seeker is able to make obvious the power of his Will. He ensures that his Will is stronger – really far stronger, than his senses. He is able to transcend the demands of his physical sheath, his emotions and his intellect.

Empowered by life force, he exercises his Will for a motionless posture or *asana*. Under the guidance of an experienced teacher, the seeker is taught to direct the mind to watch the breath. Next the seeker is taught to enter the divine cave in the brain and the spinal cord. With every moment that passes, he gets closer to his inner centre. Overtime, he or she becomes increasingly aware that one can watch, see, hear and feel the presence of God in the silence of the divine cave. This happens with every breath one takes.

Intense concentration or *dharana* is necessary for the mind and intellect to advance deeper into the divine cave. The body-mind-intellect can't be allowed to rule the seeker's Will. When the seeker is focusing on the *kutastha* in the cave, causal habits lose their grip and make progressively less demands.

Once Man becomes more aware of breath entering-leaving-stalling within the divine cave, this concentration merges with the silence during the pauses while still in the *kutastha* between the two eyebrows. Enduring here for long periods, the grace of a teacher will one day allow one to view the silence in this stillness. Here the whole universe appears as the universal organism in all beings. He becomes acutely aware of his connection with the great Cosmic Life-form of *Prakriti-Purusha* combined in pure Conscious Awareness. This is self-realisation.

Yoga

Yoga, practised with sincerity, can unite the self with the Self. Most often, Man seeks God because of pain the individualistic self suffers. Although unaware of it, Man is looking for the Bliss of God. And pain, suffering or other limits are reminders of Man's identification with his body and mind. These make him blind to the existence of his own innate state of Bliss. This agitation can take the forms of pleasure or pain, hot or cold, white or black, good or bad, likes or dislikes *[raaga-dvesha],* and so on.

Yoga un-encumbers the egoistic self by removing Man's identification with his body, mind and intellect. Man must understand that he is born of the vibrations of *AUM,* the invisible life force that upholds Creation. Until he grasps this it will be near impossible for him to enter the 'Kingdom of Heaven'. That which is born of the Spirit is pure 'Spirit'. Man must transcend the physical, the body of flesh to reach the Spirit. The seeker needs experiencing and realising, not just knowing the exercise. Such practices often take the form of dogmas and doctrines. To gain True Knowledge, one needs the mind *[manas]* and intellect *[buddhi],* memory in the *chitta* to dissociate from the sense organs. What is learned through this equipment, the *chitta,* is indirect knowledge absorbed through the senses. Eastern philosophy calls this *apara vidya.* This information is admittedly the first step to Knowledge. The second step is transformation.

Indirect knowledge is available through scriptural instruction. An experienced Master expands on it. He bases his teachings on his own intuitive experiences. However, it is the seeker's thirst for self-unfoldment that allows him to absorb such disclosures. Personal convergence with this knowledge is drawn from Man's own self-realisation. This is True Knowledge or *para vidya.* It is verified by a meticulously exacting meeting with the Self.

Man is the same perceiver-feeler-thinker [PFT] whether he looks outward at indulgence – or inward seeking the soul. There are four practical paths to set free the Body-Mind-Intellect [BMI] from Objects-Emotions-Thoughts [OET]. The seeker chooses the path that suits him best. This relies on his innate mental and intellectual tendencies *[vasanas].* His wants, the writings and happenings he will come across will also match his need.

This, of course, is no accident. In Nature, there are no accidents. Everything happens, as it should.

Spiritual Paths or The Science of Yoga

To the ignorant, the body is real. To the learned, the ego is real. To a scientist, the Law of Nature is real. To a spiritual seeker, nothing is real.

The seeker chooses to enlighten his *chitta* with *yoga.* He philosophically identifies the self with the Self or *Brahman.* By controlling his wilful wavering mind through *yoga,* the seeker merges his individual will with Cosmic Will. This allows him to create constant unity with *Brahman* in every breath and activity.

Yoga remains the most important form of spiritual exercise or *sadhana.* On a physical plane, it ensures good health and mobility. On a mental plane, it frees thought imbalance through concentration or *dharana.* On an intellectual plane, *yoga* promises freedom from delusion, and from repeated birth and death. Free from religious doctrine or discipline, *yoga* is non-sectarian by nature. Its techniques are scientific and enforced by the personal experiences of sages for centuries. The science of *yoga* offers four primary paths of spiritual exercise:

GYANA YOGA, the path of Knowledge, communicates that God is everywhere and in everything. Through *gyana yoga,* Man receives insight into the individualistic self or Ego and objects of the world. Gradually, Man frees his Awareness from the awareness of body and mind, an evolutionary need. With the help of a *guru,* Man distances himself from things and beings. He does this to arrive at a unity between the Self and God. He begins to experience God in everything and everywhere.

BHAKTI YOGA underlines devotion to an Ideal, in a spirit of intense Love. Man chants a specific *mantra,* which allows the embodied soul to unite with the deity of his choice. These chanting sounds produce vibrations in the physical and astral worlds. When such synchronising is complete then absorbed mind merges with the Cosmic Mind's vibration. Man is drawn into the realms of Eternal Love. Seeing and listening is divine because he has learned to switch off his physical body.

HATHA YOGA, which is practised in the West as 'yoga', deals with improving the body and mind. Its goal is to control the body and mind through *asanas* [body postural control], *pranayama* [breath stabilisation], *bandhas* [physical exercises] and *mudras* [symbols of worship]. Practitioners of this path begin their *yoga* by removing physical obstacles, through exercises. They are aimed at mastering the physical body and the restless breath. The mind becomes capable, gradually. By enjoying perfect union of the body and mind, he merges with the Ideal.

KARMA YOGA is reciprocity between action and reaction through the practice of detachment. When Man launches any action selflessly, it yields in him a sense of indifference and detachment from the result. Selfless action ensures *yoga* or union with God, which is the goal of Self-realisation. After that, every act is spiritual, since the motive is pure worship. Serving one's own family expands into serving the family of the world, with a sense of love and devotion to the Cosmic Whole.

Raja Yoga, also sometimes called *KriyaYoga,* is a combination of these four pure paths. It starts with *hatha yoga* to tame the physical sheath. Then, through *gyana yoga,* it tames the mental and intellectual sheaths. In all, the seeker undergoes eight stages of self-transformation and soul unfoldment. The sage Patanjali described these practices. *Kriya Yoga* is *ashtanga yoga* or the eight-limbed *yoga.*

The learned in India have practiced *ashtanga yoga* since

time immemorial. By mastering the eight steps, they have freed themselves of self-ignorance and delusions. Their spiritual attainment is supported by a firm foundation of austerity of *yama* and adherence to pledges of restraint *[niyama]*,. In- depth study of the scriptures and surrender is encouraged also.

Raja Yoga, the essence of all the four yoga paths, incorporates the *maha mudra* technique [to stabilise nerves] of *hatha yoga,* but avoids the wholly physical exercises. It also includes *pranayama* [breath control], *pratyahara* [withdrawal of the senses], *dharana* [concentration], *dhyana* [meditation uninterrupted] and *samadhi* [absorption]. The practitioner watches, looks, hears and feels the radiance and sound vibrations of God-Consciousness.

TANTRA YOGA, which has recently become popular in the West, grants the seeker with *siddhis* or psychic-powers. It is *Devi* [or Mother Spirit] worship and is an integral part of eastern philosophy. In fact, *Shaktism* is one of eastern philosophy's most important systems. *Tantra* is not witchcraft, some mysterious formulas or magic spells. These are scriptural practices based on fundamental ideas and correct reasons. Only a *tantric guru* has the knowledge of this path. And a student of *tantra* must be endowed with faith, purity, dispassion and dedication to a *guru.* The absence of these qualities in a student leads him to misuse *Shaktism.* The student must approach the subject with humility, courage, truth, contentment and Cosmic Love.

The Goal of spirituality is to assert the Infinite can't be described or defined in words. The Path is not easy to spell out. Scriptures and the Masters can show the direction. But Man himself has to rise beyond Body-Mind-Intellect.

The Eight Steps

1. Through *YAMA* or self-control [noninjury, truthfulness, noncovetousness, continence in thought, word and deed].

2. Through *NIYAMA* or moral observances [contentment, austerity, scriptural study, and surrender to God] the seeker gains detachment and mental peace. He develops compassion for all beings and creatures. Under the guidance of a *guru,* he learns to uphold *asanas* [correct physical postures] for long spans of time.
3. Through proficiency of *ASANA,* the seeker rises above physical consciousness and enters the Mind. Freed from physical restlessness, his erect spine allows awareness to flow to the lower spiritual centres or *chakras.* Gradual evolution allows awareness to move up the spine and into the brain. The main ingredient of *Raja Yoga,* also called the royal path, is *pranayama* [the science of breath control]. This is the science of controlling total cosmic power.
4. Through *PRANAYAMA,* the seeker is able to control the frequency and depth of respiration, the pulse rate, and thoughts in the Body-Mind-Intellect [BMI].
5. Then, *PRATYAHARA* allows the candidate to withdraw his senses and mind from the world of Objects-Emotions-Thoughts [OET].
6. The practitioner stops to be the Perceiver-Feeler-Thinker [PFT] and is now single-pointedly able to concentrate *[DHARANA]* within his own withdrawn mind.
7. In unbroken concentration or *DHYANA,* the practitioner intuitively experiences God as an idea.
8. In *SAMADHI,* however, he gains union with God.

Kriya Yoga

Kri is Action. Directing Man to engage in his daily actions and duties to his life and family is his *dharma.* *'Ya'* is God, who lives as the invisible witnessing *Purusha* [Spirit] in Man's visible body or *Prakriti* [Nature]. It is the power vested in *Prakriti* as *prana* or breath that allows all action. *Prakriti* delivers enlivening energy to the five senses and five organs of action. And *Yoga* is the technique of uniting the physical with the invisible sheaths *[koshas]* of Man. *Kriya Yoga* is based on inhalation. Physiologically, the technique is based on a slowing of the rate of inhalation and its gradual deepening, until the mind withdraws from the senses and is at rest. Once the mind is tranquil and full attention is withdrawn into the *kutastha* – behind and between the two eyebrows, above the cradle [sella turcica] of the pituitary gland - respiration automatically slows.

Thus, slower respiration and pulse lead to an awakening of the spiritual centres within the divine cave, the altar of God. The divine cave's magnetisation allows Man to overcome wants, habits and instinctive tendencies.

Many are of the conviction that *Kriya Yoga* and *Raja Yoga* described in the *Bhagavad Gita* are identical. In the nineteenth century, however, an esteemed philosopher, the everlasting Babaji Maharaj, reinstated the technique of *KriyaYoga* to the world. Babaji called on Shyam Charan Lahiri [1828-1895], one of his prized disciples from an antecedent birth, to the Himalayan foothills. Babaji commanded Lahiri to spread the technique of *Kriya Yoga* in India. Although Lahiri [also known as Lahiri Mahasaya] was a householder and an accountant at the British Indian Railways, he was already practicing *KriyaYoga.* His past recollection of the technique and experience guided his present life. He knew that pleasures of the senses make Man ignorant of Reality. Man forgets that divine light illumining Man's body. In Colonial India he witnessed Man wanting to rule over others, at all cost. He knew through experience that delusion and ignorance led Man to misbehave and ignore the Invisible Doer of all circumstances.

Lahiri, however, had experienced this Invisible Doer. He revelled in his inner calmness of joy and bliss. Through perseverance and intense practice of *Kriya Yoga,* Lahiri enjoyed perfect health even in old age. Even his daily mundane tasks were made efficient through inspired creativity. With devotion and concentration, Lahiri remained with his family and fulfilled his duties. All the while he practiced *Kriya Yoga* every day. He arrived at a balanced mind, with peace reigning in the family and true friendships with neighbours and co-workers. Lahiri always focused on breath control. This slowly freed him of desire and attachment. He finally saw God in everything. He treated his human encasement as a field for cultivation. Through spiritual exercises *[sadhana]*, he cultivated his bodily field to be as dynamic as possible. Here with his physical encasement he sought Immortality within himself.

Lahiri also taught *Kriya Yoga.* Among his many disciples was Priya Nath Karar [1855-1936], a widower and renunciant. Ordained Swami Yukteshwar, Karar wrote a commentary on Truth. He identified the misinformation in humanity. In 1894 he first wrote a commentary on the similarities of all religions in *The Holy Science.* He also resolutely integrated Kriya Yoga with the Karar Ashram, on the seashores of Puri in Orissa in 1903.

Swami Vivekananda [1863-1902], the first Indian to address the Parliament of Religions on Hinduism in 1893 [in Chicago, USA], predicted the arrival of another *yogi.* This one would lay the foundations of spiritualism in the Western world. He predicted there would be harmony among all religions in the world. He also predicted this *yogi* would popularise *Vedantic* culture in the West. In the same year, a male child, who was named Mukunda Lal, was born to Bhagavati Charan Ghose, a Railways employee. Ghose was one of Lahiri's disciples. Lahiri Mahasaya predicted a divine child would be born to Ghose. This child would be a student of Swami Yukteshwar.

Under the tutelage of Swami Yukteshwar, this child hastened his journey to God through the practice of meditation. He was received into the ministry as Swami Yogananda [1893–1952]. Armed with the *Kriya Yoga* technique, he was commanded to promote the principle in the West. Swami Yogananda travelled extensively. He set up several monasteries in the USA. In 1920, he founded the Self Realization Fellowship. Over his lifetime, he admitted thousands into *Kriya Yoga.*

Swami Yukteshwar also introduced Robindranath Bhattacharya [1907-2002] into *Kriya Yoga.* Ordained Swami Hariharananda, he was admitted into higher *Kriya* techniques by Swami Yogananda. In 1951 Swami Yogananda empowered Swami Hariharananda to introduce sincere seekers into *KriyaYoga.* Swami Hariharananda remained at the Karar Ashram in Puri until after Swami Yukteshwar's physical death.

In 1974, Swami Hariharananda was urged by devotees from the West to introduce them to *KriyaYoga.* At the age of 67 years, he introduced *Kriya Yoga* in Europe. By 1975, he had brought the technique to the USA, Canada and South America. He also set up the Kriya Yoga Institute in Homestead, near Miami, Florida. Here he encouraged seekers to adopt a simple lifestyle and taught them the theory and practice of *Kriya Yoga.*

Among the monks who passed on *Vedantic* culture globally was the learned scholar Swami Chinmayananda [1916-1993]. Born as Balakrishna Menon, he crisscrossed the world for fifty years, reviving the science of meditation. Twenty-five years before Swami Hariharananda brought *Kriya*

Yoga to the West, Swami Chinmayananda's speeches on Soul Culture, through the study of the *Bhagavad Gita* and the *Upanishads,* were reaching people of all ethnic backgrounds. His teaching and sermons were in English. He therefore reached people who didn't understand *Sanskrit* or any of the languages of the Indian continent.

Armed with this knowledge many seekers have studied the technique of *Kriya Yoga.* For the last twenty-five years monasteries are firmly incorporated in Europe, Britain, USA and India, especially in Orissa. Seekers from all over the world spend time at the Puri ashram to study *Vedanta* and practice *Kriya Yoga* under the scholarship of Swami Prajnanananda, Shuddhananda, and Brahmananda. The monks visit individual cities in Canada, USA and South America to meet with seekers who practice this meditation. Babaji is still at work for the last two centuries.

Prana is the Breath of Life

PRANA, at the risk of oversimplification, is the life principle and breath of Awareness. It is one with the real Self, Soul or *atma.* It is the vibrating enlivening life-force that fills the Cosmic universe at all levels, be it spiritual, physical, mental, sexual and so on. It is *AUM* the Holy Spirit, and Her power that permeates everything. It is the medicine in herbs, the nourishing power of moonlight, the fuel in food, the digestive fire satisfying appetites and the healthy lifespan in Creation. It is the breath of life of all. It enlivens the energy in every plant, creature and being in the universe.

Prana or life force can't live by itself. That is, it can't achieve its craft and vocation without the presence of the energetic essence of Matter [earth, water, fire, air and space]. Transformation into a material object is a presentation or an expression by *prana* with Matter. Some thinkers call the act of enlivenment *mahaprana* or 'The Great Animation'.

Mahaprana, therefore, contains **particles of life** held together as blissful existence with a modicum of knowledge. It can be in any form - plant, creature or Man. During meditation and the practice of *pranayama* or breath control, Man experiences this scattered animation in its unified form. He realises his true and real identity among all. This realisation - that 'he is infinite' - helps him understand that he doesn't have a fragmented existence.

Philosophically defined, *prana* is the astral life-force or AUM or the Holy Spirit or the Virgin Mother that enlivens energy and gives birth to everything. Although within the body it is a single force, it is defined as being divided into five units to heighten physical activity. They are *prana* in the chest, *apana* in the anorectal area, *samana* in the umbilical area, *udana* in the neck and *vyana* in the entire body. The first three have supreme value in the practice of *yoga.* When the upward-moving positive and downward-moving negative *prana* are balanced equity or *samana* exists. When the mind undulates with restless *prana* or breath, it is uneasy, judgmental, and active. But when *prana* and *apana* reach harmony, there is **Stillness** in *sattva.* The Self begins to show itself in the blossoming as the **Silence** of a witnessing mind, in the *kutastha.* Sages believe the mind originates with respiration and is freed with controlled respiration *[pranayama].*

Medically defined, *prana* is the physiological enlivening energy that supports all of the body through the autonomic, sensory and motor nervous systems through *nadis.* The sympathetic nervous system *[pingala]* is the most autonomously restless *[rajas],* while the parasympathetic nervous system *[ida]* is the most lethargic *[tamas].* When the two are quiet, the energy that flows through the spinal cord *[sushumna]* is harmonious *[sattva]* and receptive to spiritual activity. These three channels - *pingala, ida* and *sushumna* - within the spinal cord need to be cleared of restlessness. Depending on the seeker's evolution, the life force flows contrarily within these astral channels.

The first two - *pingala* and *ida* - are interconnected at different levels within the spine. When separated from each other during intensive meditation, the third channel, or *sushumna,* is cleared of the debris of Man's past and present. *Prana* then flows freely, and Man can move from restlessness to introverted stillness and silence.

Prana is also described as the vibrating creative Light-Energy - of the Unmanifest *Shakta-Shakti.* This combined *Purusha-Prakriti* merging is that of Awareness in Consciousness. *Purusha* silently witnesses and permeates all with energy. *Prakriti's* Awareness underlines and supports and enlivens everything in unmanifest Energy. As Awareness, She is the infrastructure of every atom. And as Nature, She looks to the affairs of the universe - birth, nourishment and dissolution of Creation, both in the macrocosm and the microcosm.

Together they are Universal Intelligence or Christ or Krishna. They become visible to the reflecting seeker in the *kutastha.* Here the Father is visible as the Son and vice versa – all born of a virgin mother.

All Creation, thus, is an exhibition through *prana,* the power of God. In the macrocosm, *prana* is both a spiritual energy and life force. In the microcosm, *prana* enlivens the biological body. It controls the astral body with five kinds of breath: *prana, apana, samana, udana* and *vyana* [respiration, excretion, digestion, inspiration and circulation, respectively]. The Self draws in breath with the power of God *[Sa or So].* The power is in the *kutastha* above the pituitary and behind the eyebrows. Here, oxygen is altered to *prana* or life force to nourish the body *[ham].*

Prana is *AUM* [or *Amen* or *Amin* or *Hum].* It silently enlivens every atom and molecule in us and in the universe.

To gain self-control over this innate energy, one needs a *guru* to show the 'what, where and how'. Through the mantra of *'hum sa - so hum'* Man is taught to tap into the source of God's rejuvenating power. He watches the breath, he looks at the *kutastha* for the appearance of the *vishwa rupa,* he hears the symphony of *Aum,* he tastes the nectar dripping at the uvula, and he feels *prana* in every breath. The experience decodes the implicit meaning of *AUM* in meditation.

When the seeker succeeds in erasing his extroverted existence in meditation, he sees the reflecting image of God in his *kutastha.* He loses all sense of the physical body [or 'M' of *AUM].* He, then, hears vibrating of the astral body [or 'U' of *AUM].* He has entered his super-consciousness. Finally, he hears the sound of the causal body [or 'A' of *AUM].* Then, he hears the high-pitched sound of many waters emanating from the soul and from all around him. He has found *AUM.* He reaches the fabric and invisible infrastructure of Creation. This is the real Knowledge of the Soul. Once the seeker familiarises with this sound, he first follows this inner symphony. He patiently watches all his actions and infers he is energised and powered by *AUM.* He finally realises he does nothing.

Sadhana or Spiritual Effort

Life is a journey. It is a pilgrimage to fulfil life's purpose. Its goals are duty or *Dharma* of desire for fulfilment or *Kama.* They come first. Discovering and introducing human birth with meaning, objective and wealth comes next as *artha.* Experiencing liberation from the wheel of birth and death or *moksha* is the final goal of a human birth. Human life is a battle to regain peace, tranquillity and true happiness. Conflicts of existence are born in our social lives, in our family, our workplace and in the world. Inner conflicts and values contradict moral values and ideals. In this struggle, Man is victimised by negativity and forced to make unwanted compromises. He becomes a victim of want, anger, greed, jealousy, hypocrisy and possessiveness. After carrying out the first two goals, Man re-evaluates life and realises he needs permanent happiness because that is his eternal nature. He embarks on his spiritual journey looking to rise above simple biological existence and searching for inner tranquillity and spiritual emancipation.

Without a map and an experienced guide, a spiritual journey is difficult. Though scriptural text is the map, it is often difficult to decipher without an experienced teacher. The chosen Master should have made the journey himself. To transform Man, the path must be lit up with true spiritual knowledge and revelation of Truth, as opposed to material knowledge. Putting spiritual knowledge to practice is *sadhana.* The experience of *sadhana* is the result of a life of self-discipline and meditation.

During their spiritual effort, seekers come up with issues. Some feel their progress is too slow. Some feel a sense of bewilderment. Some endure a sense of loneliness. Some are troubled by experiences of phenomenon during deep meditation. Others feel they've slipped backwards. But these feelings are often a result of failure to endure by the *yama* and *niyamas* [the do's and don'ts] of personal conduct. To direct a wavering seeker through the forests of temptation, restlessness and emotional weakness, a *guru* is essential. Surges of inner awakening until now unknown energy within the seeker are signs of progress. A teacher must be there to guide the student through hurdles. Regulated slow breathing, as taught by the *guru*, combats fears of falling into a void.

The biological human body is like a chariot. The Soul is the charioteer. The five senses are horses that draw the chariot. When driven by the egoistic individualised self, the horses pull in different directions. For a spiritual journey, the body and the senses must be healthy, well trained and under control of Universal Intelligence. The transforming individualistic self needs the grace of the witnessing Consciousness and the will of Nature's Awareness. The self, in turn, must agree to the teachings of an experienced *guru*. Well-versed in the art of self-control and self-unfoldment the teacher takes the self to submit to the Self for gradual

Raging Conflicts in Spiritual Life

The individualistic self is the Ego or *ahankar*. It is the non-evolved *chitta* or the combined oblivious personality of mind, intellect and ego. The individualistic mortal is the *jiva* or self. The real doer of all actions through the mind, intellect, senses and the ego, is the soul or *atma* or Self. A spiritual journey is about transforming the ignorant, individualistic personality into an evolved *chitta*.

The biological human body is composed of three bodies: gross physical or *sthula sharira,* astral or *sukshma sharira* and causal or *karana sharira.* The gross physical body is perishable, and is discarded to merge with the Cosmic Elements of *Prakriti.* The physiological-psychological astral body is comprised of *Pranic* energy. The causal body is made up of the essence *Aum* of both the physical and astral. This biological body, of twenty-four units, is both the path of extroverted ignorance, and of introverted emancipation.

To ensure self-unfoldment, the biological body has to be trained and composed. Spiritual seekers prevail, but because of raging conflicts in disposition, few flourish. Seekers themselves can be arranged into three kinds. First are those who study the scriptures for knowledge. Second are those who study the scriptures for their historical correctness. And three, there are those who practice the truths of the scriptures and personally experience the scriptural subtleties.

THE TWENTY- FOUR UNITS OF BIOLOGICAL BODY

Five elements

[earth, water, fire, air and space]

Five *pranic* subtle counterparts

[smell, taste, shape, touch and sound]

Five senses of perception

[nose, tongue, eyes, ears and skin]

Five organs of action

[legs, arms, speech, organs of generation and excretion]

Mind

Intellect

Ego

Memory of past personality or

Chitta

All scriptures insist on training in Soul Culture. This consists of the art of self-control, self-unfoldment and Self-realisation. The last, Self-realisation, is only possible through *yoga,* the art of uniting the individualistic self with the Cosmic Self. This is the *yoga* of meditation. A *yogic* life of moderation, in such indulgences as food, sex, sleep and social dependency, lessens mental and intellectual restlessness. While extroversion recedes there is a gradual inner detachment. This ensures self-control and inner self-mastery. This also leads to an integration of the outer lifestyle. There is a new-found inner harmony. There is, in effect, an automatic tendency to do the 'right' thing. This inner transformation divinises all actions. Fresh intuitive knowledge dawns through personal experience. It is the Self that is 'the doer' of all his actions. Over time and with sincere effort, the ego's stubborn hold on the *chitta* personality relaxes. Devotion to the Cosmic Whole becomes obvious in the harmonisation of all internal and external action.

Fixed in the wisdom of personal experience and confirmed through meditation, a spiritual seeker begins to understand life as it presents itself. This is the path that integrates the biological body's actions with the spiritual body's natural urges.

There are many that aspire to a spiritual life but balk at the idea of its legality. They eventually fail even to embark on a spiritual journey. Their primary question: "If the Invisible God lives within us always, why can't we see Him?" most teachers are likely to answer: "He lives within the divine cave of the spinal cord and brain and is the doer of all action, visible or unseen. But to find Him, Man must trudge through the jungles of the biological body. He must carve out pathways through the thickets of old habits. He must nourish and reclaim valuable unused wastelands. Only then will he reach the path of meditation towards the brain, and into the *kutastha* where He can be found".

The invisible body's extrovert nature deludes us. It pushes us towards materialism. Desires and wants impregnated during previous births continue to plague Man. They drive our extrovert natures through the senses, organs of action, the mind and intellect. Like quicksand, it pulls us into *maya.* With that comes our ignorance of her. Deluded by tendencies we make mistakes. In fact, a survey found that though most people believe in God, they are far too engrossed in the materialistic world to search for answers. They can't make out that everything around them is animated by His power.

The H
the ove
you
enters
entirely
sperm
twelve
Secure
body, ma
seat of
for Ma
(prana)
mature

Th
marrow
Each of
plexuses
all physi
a specif

Th
instrum
The ast
physical
brain a
the astr
direct
though
other pl

Chakras, the Centres of Energy

The Human Body, they say, is a miniature universe. A look at the organisation of Man's body reveals its perfection. It is as you can see, detailed for a divine plan. The Soul *[purusha]* enters Matter *[prakriti]* as a spark of consciousness. Life force enlivens the incipient organism as soon as there is union of sperm with ovum. As the embryo develops over the next twelve weeks, it develops into the seat of a coming soul. Securely fixed within the medulla of the brain, this person's body, mind and intellect now grow to maturity. Here, in the seat of a future being, the individual self *[or chitta]* remains for Man's lifetime. Empowered by the creative life force *[prana]* the foetus advances through distinct stages into a mature human body.

The body, made up chiefly of skin, flesh, bones, fat, marrow, blood and nerves, originates from the five elements. Each of these has a different 'throne' in the body. Called plexuses these 'thrones' are also called *chakras.* They perform all physical work for the body. These seats of power also have a specific relation with the physical body.

The Soul's Creativity is obvious through astral and causal instruments. The astral instrument is empowered by *prana.* The astral body has the power to enliven the energy of the physical body. The main generators of power are the astral brain and the six astral centres or plexuses *[chakras]* along the astral spinal cord *[sushumna].* The causal instrument directs the body with memories of past habits through thoughts. Besides the medulla *[ajna chakra],* there are five other plexuses or *chakras* coursing down the spinal cord:

- The cervical, opposite the throat *[vishuddha chakra].*

- The thoracic, opposite the heart *[anhaata chakra].*
- The lumbar, opposite the navel *[manipura chakra].*
- The sacral plexus, opposite the organs of reproduction *[svadhisthana chakra].*
- The coccygeal plexus, at the base of the spine below the anus *[muladhara chakra].*

Since the plexuses are also composed of the five elements, the three qualities or *gunas* of Matter – Tamas, Rajas and Sattva [inertia, creativity and harmony] – govern them. Although the coarser works of the body need the lower five spinal physical plexuses, the finer roles of the Soul - awareness, intelligence, will and feeling - need the medulla and the brain. This is where the subtle centres of different states of awareness [awake, dream and deep sleep] lie. The centres of super-consciousness [for Universal Intelligence and for Cosmic Consciousness] also lie here.

The centre for Universal Intelligence lies in the *kutastha* behind the two eyebrows, in the frontal brain within the thalamus. It is a reflection of the medullary centre, *[ajna chakra].* It is seen as the third eye of Awareness and Consciousness in meditation. The other centre of super-consciousness, for Cosmic Consciousness, lies at the vertex of the brain *[sahasrahara chakra]* and far down into the pineal gland. When a Soul descends below the pineal and through the *chakras* into body consciousness, a cosmic delusion or Maya influences it. Individual delusion or *avidya* allows the Soul to forget its divine origin. The individualistic self or *chitta* now identifies itself with Man's body, his relatives and his possessions. The Self ascribes to itself all the physical body's limits and the influence of Nature's qualities *[gunas].*

The physical body is a field of external action. Inert *[tamasic guna]* Matter is enlivened by *pranic* inspiration *[rajasic guna]* to create the restless active man and the ever-changing world he strives, ineffectively, to control.

The cerebrospinal axis, with its six *chakras* of life and

awareness [coccygeal, sacral, lumbar, thoracic, cervical and medullary], acts from two magnetic poles. The mind *[manas]* drives Man's faculties outward through these centres. It keeps the motor and sensory roles of the body actively extroverted. The spinal axis is in a mode of creativity *[rajas]*. The intellect *[buddhi]* retires inwards. It becomes absorbed with subtle inner supra-mental forces and faculties. The qualities of Nature in this part of the cerebrospinal axis, that is, the cervical plexus, are in harmony *[sattva]*. When Man has successfully freed the thoracic plexus from the overpowering tendencies of me and mine, tranquillity influences Man.

The area above the medulla and the pituitary, with its astral centres, is the Soul's home. This part of the brain upholds all bodily fields and is the source of forces that create and keep Man's physical, astral and causal bodies. It is also the route through which forces of the Soul leave the three bodies *[shariras]* and return to the Spirit.

From these nerve centres, *yogis* experience different grades of spiritual revelation. Matching grades of physical sensations are the result of deep concentration. The experience of Nature's powers within the cerebrospinal axis takes the seeker's self through the three unified nerve channels *[ida, pingala* and *sushumna]* and into the hypothalamus. Extinction of the self's individuality results in the Self absorbing the self, in the thalamus. This knowledge, coursing through the six mystical *chakras,* is a direct personal experience of pure Awareness.

Though Man's awareness is eternally clouded with impressions, the aim is not only to satisfy the desires of the senses but also further the Soul's emancipation. The medullary centre is both the centre of all autonomic bodily functions and the habitat of personality, the *chitta* [mind-intellect-ego complex].

Man, cloaked in delusion, is characterised by mental restlessness. All this is because of ingrained tendency within the five lower *chakras*. The coccygeal centre leads Man into a deluded love of money and, thus, greed for wealth. The sacral centre services sexual indulgence with wasting of primal energy fluid or *ojas*. The lumbar centre is preoccupied with cravings of food or taste and wasteful social pastime. The thoracic centre remains preoccupied with me and mine, while the cervical centre is wrapped up in egoistic pride and self-value.

Most people work from the three lower *chakras* for wealth, sex and food. Introduced into this activity through need for protecting and preserving themselves and their families, Man becomes habituated to overreaction and indulgence. Much of these leanings are instilled. Parents, peers, culture or circumstance inculcate these habits. This lifestyle leaves no time to learn about the existence of God.

These children grow up engrossed in materialism. And though many of them are intelligent, powerful, educated, scientifically gifted and dignified, their individualised ego leads them to rationalism. They are sure there is no God.

Most love or crave flattery, and keep bad company. Thus distracted, they cannot hear the Soul's reclusive call. They do not yearn for Soul realisation. A youth nurtured to be a nonbeliever of God becomes addicted to indulgence. He grows up gregarious. He speaks too much and seeks aggrandizement and crudity. His mind and his company match the restlessness of his personality. Then there are parents who are spiritually educated. But they are unable or do not know how to teach their progeny. These children cannot see or hear the prompting of the Soul.

Pranic energy is stored in the lower *chakras* to energise speech, breath and desires. He, who accomplishes surpassing these faculties, has the ability to raise the energy from the coccygeal to the pituitary plexus. Only such a one can unveil the mystery of the universe. His intuitive knowledge banishes worldly darkness and the individuality of the self. He is able to dwell in the sixth *chakra*. Here he witnesses and sees the luminous centre of the *kutastha.* He hears the mystical sound of *AUM and* feels the breath of life. He has risen above the pituitary gland and is freed from the influence of *maya* or delusion through transcendence.

Central Nervous System and Universal Consciousness

The Human Brain is the mightiest of God's creations. It is the altar where *Brahma's* creative power enlivens the twenty-four essences in the causal being. Through the medulla, pituitary and the hypothalamic glands, the solar sympathetic *[pingala]* and lunar parasympathetic channels *[ida]* are flooded with *pranic* energy. These channels descend through the midbrain and the pons. The brainstem now links the thalamus with the pineal gland, cerebellum, medulla and the regions below. Through the spinal cord *[sushumna]* and nerve bundles the physical body connects with the divine cave.

Sushumna is the ladder, and the lone path, by which Man can reach the altar of God in the brain. He climbs every rising step through meditation. The spinal cord's nerves are the only means whereby various parts of the body and the mind can be enlivened, energised and rejuvenated. A gradual transformation of the physical *[sthula sharira]* and of the astral bodies *[sukshma sharira]* starts. From the tips of the fingers to the core of one's being, an awakening of latent powers lying dormant begins. Through meditation, Man is able to withdraw the life force or *prana [pratyahara]*. From special senses, as well as organs under the control of the motor, sensory, sympathetic and parasympathetic nervous systems awareness is withdrawn.

The spinal cord becomes isolated as a magnetised axis of the physical body. The medulla *[ajna chakra]* works as the positive pole, and the coccygeal plexus *[muladhara chakra]* is the negative post. Special breathing exercises of breath control *[pranayama]* are taught. They magnetise and energize the spinal cord. In this state of *dharana* – deep in concentration and introverted – Man experiences subtle sensations of sight and sound with increasing Awareness. Once centred *[dhyana],* after many tries under the guidance of a teacher, he is ready for Self-realisation.

Being awarded with the most chance of life after death, only Man has the ability to experience God. When it happens He is experienced as the all-pervasive Spirit within himself and in the universe. He knows to reach his goal of self-unfoldment and Self-realisation in this lifetime he must remain in the *kutastha.* He realises he is the master of his own destiny. Through the power of meditation and *yoga,* he can determinedly transform his body matter. Through harnessing Cosmic Will even the DNA shape of every neuro-transmitter and neuro-hormone is altered. Hormones released from these master glands [pituitary and hypothalamus] in the brain now change the works of every cell in the body, as wanted by Man.

With progressive transformation permanently etched in the centre of awareness in the thalamus the power of Will in the forebrain controls all master glands for continued evolution. The medulla spreads spiritualised life force into every cell of the body. Gradually, Man begins to feel his own existence. Over time and with training under an experienced mentor, Man transforms into an intuitive spiritual being. He becomes an instrument of increasing perfection through increasing integration. He uses his life force. He commits it through meditation. He makes it an instrument of God's power and love.

For this to be possible, Man has to train himself through the different paths of *yoga.* For Self-realisation he needs knowledge, including that of the scriptures. Armed with it he experiences universal assertions. To experience the Divine, an expanding awareness and merging into cosmic consciousness through meditation is the necessary path. Spiritual Truths personally discovered are then experienced.

Preliminary physical, psychological and intellectual training helps. Peeling off layers of past births that encase the individualised self is necessary. And, of course, this is all a gradual process.

But when Man's *sadhana* nudges him, he intuitively and instinctively knows he has reached the doors of self-unfoldment. The consequent realisation of Self will and does happen. He now merges his Awareness with Consciousness. It happens in the depths of his brain, at the altar of God *[samadhi]*.

The Mind as an Organ of the Body

The Mind, as an inner organ of thought, within the divine cave is *antakarana*. It is also called the *chitta*. It is functioning at three levels:

Logic and reasoning as *buddhi* or intellect;

Emotion or sensory mind or *manas;*

Ego or pseudo-soul or *ahankara;*

The Mind, as *manas, buddhi* and *ahankara,* is made up of atomic physical matter. All is born of nutrients or food, from Nature. It has the atomic structure of creation. Because Mind is Matter, it can focus on only one thought at a time. This allows us to direct thought in a specific narrow direction at any given moment. Result is an attachment to certain points of view. However, like an aura, the mind can pervade also. It penetrates an entire field of understanding, despite its atomic nature.

The outgoing biological mind is unstable, constantly changing in space as well as in time. But in reality, it is only a series of thoughts that shift continually, both from the point of focus, as well as in ideas. Because the mind is subtle, the seeker must devote intense attention to it, especially in spiritual effort or *sadhana.* Watching its movements gives insight into what causes internal thoughts. It also helps identify all external thought stimuli. Meditation helps detect all unrestrained estimate of mind's volatility. Man understands why it is so difficult to discipline. Despite that, in the *yoga* of meditation, mind control is of supreme importance. The inability to achieve this allows Mind to lose direction over a person's body, mind and intellect. This leads to the sorrow of disease or discomfort. Restraint of the mind through meditation, on the other hand, results in harmony between bodily energy and life force.

Patanjali, the philosopher who described the eight-fold path of *Ashtanga* or *Raja Yoga,* recognised and outlined the Mind's four levels of work:

- As the unconscious *chitta,* or feeling blind awareness of the mental field.
- As *manas,* or the sensory and emotional mind.
- As *ahamkara* of self-conscious intellectual thought, or 'I' am 'Me'.
- As *buddhi,* or intelligence, or 'I am I'.

According to Patanjali, the mental field of the unenlightened *chitta* serves as a general backdrop to biological awareness. Within it, is the unconscious mind of the causal state. Embedded in it are all its memories and tendencies amassed over past reincarnations. *Chitta* as 'personality' exists in all of Nature - both in the animate and in the inanimate. It is responsible for the autonomic and spontaneous roles of the body. It is the automatic trigger for all organic structure. It directs the operatives of the entire Cosmos. It is answerable for the physiological and psychological roles of the Total Mind, of which we are unaware. Unenlightened *chitta* works as collective *unconsciousness.* It is subtly imprinted as an experience of both the body and of Nature. It functions even when Nature and the body sleep. It behaves like an organic memory. Records of the complete essence of awareness exist in it as a latent seed state.

In hypnosis, the mind-intellect is brought to the level of the unconscious *chitta.* At this level we can recall everything that has happened to us. Within it, *chitta* contains deep-seated emotions, impressions, attachments, habits and tendencies. It is, in a sense, Man's own individual fragment of Nature or *Prakriti.* Man looks at the world through the eyes of her three *gunas* [inertia, creativity, and harmony], but filtered through the screen of *chitta.* Man uses the gross and subtle bodies made up of the combined *tattvas* or five element principles [earth, water, fire, air and space] to fulfil his wants.

The sensory and emotional mind of our personal Subconscious-Awareness is called *manas*. It is comprised of two parts, the senses and the organs of action. The sensory mind is capable only of thoughts of desire, likes and dislikes, love and hate, emotions and imagination. It doesn't have the ability to stabilise, follow, and assimilate.

The Mind is the efferent 'limb' of the primitive animal reflex arc. It allows the 'outgoing' mind to consider 'incoming' information through the afferent arc, and coordinating it with habits and instincts from past births. The Mind is vaguely connected to Awareness. But here, it remains inarticulate. *Manas* has no principles or value systems. Through it we become enmeshed in our emotions. We become victims of our outgoing senses that present themselves as pleasures and distastes. This outgoing energy creates an inner darkness or *avidya* in our inner nature of awareness. *Manas,* as the emotional mind, cannot be transcended. It must be stilled and silenced of all thought, intellectual and emotional.

In *sadhana,* a still and silent mind is an inward movement of divine energy, moving towards the divine cave. Man concentrates *[dharana]* in the brain and spinal cord. He LOOKS for the Cosmic Vision inside the glabella [between the eyebrows]. He WATCHES the life-infusing breath coming in through the nostrils, drawn up by the *kutastha.* Within he HEARS the Cosmic sound, *AUM,* which arms the gross, subtle and causal bodies. He FEELS God's presence as breath, with every inspiration. He senses it spreading to every part of his physical body. And above all, he becomes AWARE of the ocean of Consciousness in the cave and beyond. Intuitively, he experiences 'I am Me and Me is I'.

If fortunate to have the grace of God and guru, he might taste the nectar of immortality dripping on the tongue from the uvula – straight from the collective centres of Consciousness and Awareness in the pineal reunion position.

The extrovert mind, on the other hand, uses the same energy to justify the ego as 'I am Me'. The self-conscious mind or ego *[ahankara]* is also under the influence of the *tattvas* or elements. It is characterised by conceit, pride of one's own self-image. It is the 'Me' behind all thoughts of intellectualism. It is also the cause of fragmentation of the lower and higher minds. Ego thrives on division, strife, on 'Me and Mine'. Supported by a substratum of past habits, opinions, ideas and so on, it provides energy to the reactions of the emotional mind.

The rational mind is the intellect. An individualised reflection of Awareness and Consciousness is Universal Intelligence in the *kutastha,* above the pituitary gland. It is a part of Mahat or Cosmic Intelligence. This is different from the intellect, which has the ability to rationalise. Logic allows it to separate the truth from lie, the good from the bad and the real from the unreal, through detached observation. The rational mind has the ability to change.

When directed outwards, its energy gives reality to the idea of sense, pleasure and purpose in life. Characterised by wisdom in its changed state, it does not become enmeshed in ideas of status and possession. It rejects all justification of emotions and belief. When directed inwards, its energy leads the mind towards the divine cave, the inner Spirit or Self. In time it reaches the *kutastha* at the centre of Universal Intelligence.

The individualised self or reincarnated awareness in a jiva is an individualised fragment of Cosmic Awareness-Consciousness. Evolved intellect as an individualised reflection of Universal Intelligence leads to a higher sense of identity with the Self, through gyana or self-knowledge. The 'gyana' state of the mind is the purest reflection about Reality. To experience this stage, Man needs intense spiritual practice.

The individualised self or reincarnated awareness in a jiva is an individualised fragment of Cosmic Awareness-Consciousness. Evolved intellect as an individualised reflection of Universal Intelligence leads to a higher sense of identity with the Self, through gyana or self-knowledge. The 'gyana' state of the mind is the purest reflection about Reality. To experience this stage, Man needs intense spiritual practice.

Nature Mirrored in the Human Body

Does Ice need to 'search' for water? Man searching for God would be like that. He is the microcosm within the macrocosm. Failing to understand the universe is an expression of God mirroring this unawareness. All, which is obvious, is Nature or *Prakriti* [Matter]. It is supported and witnessed by the indwelling Universal Soul or *Purusha* [Spirit]. *Prakriti* is composed of eight ingredients: earth, water, fire, air, space, mind, intellect and ego. Each self-centred part is ruled by these eightfold units of Nature. Man is firmly set up with six plexuses or *chakras* in the spinal cord and the brain. They label these eightfold parts within them. *Prakriti* has two appearances. *Para prakriti* or higher nature gifted with introverted quiet and peace. And there is *apara prakriti* or lower nature, skilled in extroverted, creative and restless qualities of materialism. The six *chakras,* including the *ajna chakra,* are part of *apara prakriti.* They are enabled with the power of *maya* or delusion.

Para prakriti stays above the pituitary and *ajna chakra* within the thalamus. It leads *apara prakriti* away from worldly bondage and towards spiritual liberation. With each breath pulled in, oxygen is circulated not only through the lungs, but is drawn into the self into the *kutastha.* Here it is altered into *Prana* to enliven the biological body.

The visible body is the cause of bondage and restlessness. The invisible body is energised and enlivened by the Soul. It directs the brain, spinal cord and nerve bundles to do what must be done for daily living - at work, play or rest. The invisible body is spiritual by nature and is the path towards self-unfoldment and Self-realisation. Without the invisible individualised self, the visible biological body can't work.

Meditation or *yoga,* by definition, is the path to free the biological body from the mind, intellect and ego. Only then can the invisible extroverted self unite with the invisible introverted Soul or Self. True, the two are intrinsically united, but the union must be experienced personally, and intuitively, in meditation.

The Astral Mind in Physiological and Psychological Bodies

PRANA is pure life-force energy. It is a mixture of awareness and electrons. The creative or *rajasic* life force, present in the embryo of a united sperm and ovum, descends into the physical and astral bodies through seven subtle energy centres. Two of these are introverted spiritual centres in the brain and five extroverted centres are in the spinal cord. Here, life force or *prana,* which is God's supremacy in the biological body, is concentrated for outward expression through the peripheral nervous system. The life-force energy is, traditionally, distinguished into five *pranas* for crystallisation, circulation, assimilation, metabolism and elimination. The outward-bound pathways are the five senses and motor-physiological-psychological services of the organs of action.

The physical body consists of a physical brain, central nerve centres [cervical, thoracic, lumbar, sacral and coccygeal] forming plexuses, and the peripheral nervous system. The deeper astral nervous system provides the physical body with an energy-based infrastructure of *prana.* This subtle astral body or *sukshma sharira* supports and nourishes the physical body or *sthula sharira* with its innate physiological-psychological life-energy.

The astral spinal channels coursing along the peripheral nervous system are called *nadis.* Channelling life force as awareness and energy through these *nadis,* they flow along commonly accepted paths. Energy to and from the divine cave of the brain and spinal cord course through special senses, autonomic nerve channels, and motor and sensory nerve fibres. The supply is to every atom, cell and organ in the body. The main astral channel of the spinal cord or *nadi* of light is the *sushumna.* It has two shiny coverings, the *vajra* and the *chitra.*

The *sushumna* is the shining astral spinal cord, which controls and connects the works of the astral centres of *tattvas* [earth, water, fire, air and space]. It extends from the coccygeal plexus to the base of the brain in the medullary centre. The extrovert coccygeal plexus or *muladhara* is the centre for money and materialism.

Covering the divine channel of the *sushumna* or spinal cord is *vajra* or the astral dura mater, which allows motor works of expansion and contraction. It extends from the sacral plexus to the brain. The extrovert sacral plexus or *svadhisthana* is the centre for sex drive and sexual appetite.

Within the *vajra* is the second astral spine - *chitra* [or arachnoid mater of the physical spinal cord]. It extends from the lumbar plexus or *manipura* to the brain. It relates to spiritual activities towards greater consciousness. The *manipura* is the centre for taste and appetite for food.

The *vajra* and *chitra* help create attachment to money, sex, and food through the lower *chakras.* The *muladhara* attaches to money. Lust originates from the navel centre or *manipura.* Indulgences spring from the *svadhisthana.* The heart or *anhaata* centre displays as attachment to family, friends, possession and wealth. The *vishuddha* or throat centre manifests as pride and arrogance. The *vajra* and *chitra* are also interconnected to the parasympathetic and sympathetic channels or *ida* and *pingala.* These cross channels obstruct the free flow of *prana* through the *sushumna.* Meditation erases these obstructive cross-channels.

The *brahmanadi* is within the *sushumna* and is lined by pia mater. The cerebrospinal fluid and life force ascends and descends from the coccygeal to the hypothalamic-pituitary centre and back. This happens in the brain flow through the *brahmanadi.* There are two other channels within the spinal cord. They are the unmoving parasympathetic *ida* and the restless creative sympathetic *pingala*. The *tamasic ida* presents Man with sloth, idleness, apathy, recklessness and procrastination. The *rajasic pingala* gives Man his creativity and ambition. The traits of selfishness, arrogance, hypocrisy, rudeness, anger, violence, ignorance, lack of introspection and extroversion are characteristics of a restless mind in the *rajas* personality.

These two *nadis* are interconnected with each other, and with the *vajra-chitra* channels, at various sites along the *sushumna*. During meditation, these cross-bridges are destroyed and the three channels *[ida, pingala* and *sushumna]* are freed of all obstacle, resulting in free-flowing *prana*.

Centred in the pineal gland, the astral brain emits rays of Awareness and Conscious Intelligence. It controls the activities of the three astral channels. Varying degrees of the power of Awareness and Intelligence are expressed. *Prana* flows through all the astral *chakras*. They display in the physical body as characteristic activities of nerve plexuses.

In Sanskrit, the term *prana* has many definitions. Translated literally, it means 'breath'. Esoterically, it is the 'breath of life' or 'life-force' or 'cosmic energy', which supports and nourishes all physical expression. Physiologically, *prana* is subdivided to identify the sheath or *kosha* it enlivens and supports. It is used as a common name for all the purposeful divisions of this power.

During meditation, the three channels are separated and the *sushumna* cleared of all obstacles. Networks crossing their path are obscured. The devotee is now free to enter the divine altar of God in the brain.

In the cervical plexus [or throat] or *vishuddha chakra*, the astral body subtly expresses itself as calm intuition. This *chakra* rules the organs of sound [the ears] and expression [mouth]. A smoky purple lotus with sixteen petals represents it. It is the seat of space and its seed symbol is *ham*. A *yogi* who concentrates on this centre can gain great wisdom, with knowledge of the highest Reality. In the physical body, the anatomical cervical plexus controls the throat, the larynx and the respiratory system. The thyroid and parathyroid glands are also under control of this nerve plexus.

The dorsal plexus [or heart] or *anhaata chakra* is found in the spine, at the level of the heart. The natural inner music of the subtle body, the 'untenanted sound' is heard at this centre. A red lotus with twelve petals represents it. It is the seat of air and its seed symbol is *yam.* The *anhaata chakra* rules the organ of skin [as touch] and the organs of action [as grasping hands]. All *prana* or life force originates at this *chakra*-respiration *[pranaya]*, excretion *[apanaya]*, circulation *[vyanaya]*, crystallisation *[udanaya]* and assimilation *[samanaya]*. A *yogi* who concentrates on this centre arrives at skilfulness over his speech and can become an ascetic. In the physical body, the dorsal nerve plexus controls the cardiovascular system and the heart plexus. Through the thymus, it also controls bodily immunity. From a psychological point, it is the site of devotion and spiritual ambition.

The lumbar plexus [or navel] or *manipura chakra* is the City of Gems. It is earned through powerful self-control while in this seat of fire. A blue lotus with ten petals represents this astral centre. Its seed symbol is *ram.* It controls the organs of taste and digestion. The organs of action of feet for movement are controlled from here. He who meditates on this centre becomes an authority on the wisdom of caring for Nature. On a physical level, *manipura chakra* is connected to the digestive system through the solar plexus. It especially relates to the functions of the small intestines and the liver. It also governs the works of the pancreas. On a psychological level, it relates to the power of personal will and ego, or 'my will'.

The sacral or pelvic plexus or *svadhisthana chakra* is the sex centre. It is found just above the root *chakra* in the coccyx. It stands for self-abode, where spiritual energy lies hidden and dormant. Represented by a vermilion lotus with six petals, it is the seat of water. Its seed symbol is *vam.* It rules the organs of the reproductive system. Its emission is the only visible bodily essence of the physical body or *ojas* that is obvious as life force. It should not be wasted in self-indulgence. Adhering to restraint can control it. *Yogis* who meditate on this *chakra* destroy inherent passion and conceit in their personalities. On a physical level, the sacral centre controls the urogenital system. It is especially related to the health of the testes and the ovaries. On a psychological level, it is the seat of sexual need of the yearning mind.

The coccygeal plexus or root or *muladhara chakra* is found at the base of the spine, just above the anus. It is the root-foundation of all the *chakras*. It is here that all energy lies dormant, until lifted towards the seventh *chakra* in the brain. Represented by a red lotus with four petals, it is the seat of earth. It is a seed symbol *lam*. It rules the organs of smell. It controls the organs of action in elimination, through the rectum, anus and bladder. Concentrating on this centre leads to earning great power through controlled speech and breath. On a spiritual level, the coccygeal plexus is where the power of restraint is harnessed. On a physical level, it controls the parasympathetic-sympathetic excretory and secretory systems. It works through the adrenal glands. It is the centre for material desire and wealth. On a psychological level, it is the site of ignorance and fear.

Masters advise Man that he must withdraw his sensory awareness away from the lowest three centres and raise it up to the *kutastha*, behind the glabella and above the pituitary, and behind and between the two eyebrows.

From that point, Man can expect to constantly experience the Soul. He looks forward to performing all his work as an instrument of God's work. Man's self-effort progresses to a spiritual evolution. There is a constant move to Soul Culture. Man can begin to see God in every happening, even those of mundane daily living.

The Causal Body

The Gross Physiological Biological Body is created from inert flesh and bone, the *tamasic* vegetative element. Born of food and passed on to Man through the mother's womb it grows within food taken in by him during his lifetime. Composed of atoms, this nourishment is, in time, returned and assimilated into the physical body of the Great Mother, the physical Universe.

The subtle astral body is intelligent life-force energy. Made up of 'LIFE-TRONS' and expressing them as *rajasic* creativity, they display as *Prana.* Breath is the umbilical cord that joins the Cosmic Mother and Man's physical expression. This *pranic* energy leaves the physical body, as the last breath, at the end of this display.

The causal body or *karanic sharira* is the subtlest. Made up of the essence of thoughts and ideas of present and past births, it is what directs Man's existence. All records of Man's physical *[tamas]* and subtle *[rajas]* bodies are embedded within its memory-seed. Here, harmony *[sattva]* exists as 'THOUGHT-TRONS', the essence of all ideas. The causal body's presence behind the physical and astral aids existence at all levels. It makes Man aware of his wish to live. This characteristic causal awareness also permeates within the already mentioned three astral spines. It courses brilliantly through the *brahmanadi* as well. The causal body serves as the mighty reservoir of Awareness-Consciousness.

The Soul is the power behind the mind that feels, the intellect that thinks and the intelligence that wills. It is allied in all their characteristics as memory. The causal brain is the ever-existing, ever-aware, ever-blissful essence of thoughts. It expresses as the individualised 'Me' or unenlightened *chitta.* As *chitta* descends into the causal nerve plexuses, it reveals as different thought-essence tendencies or *vasanas.*

The causal nerve plexus, in the pineal gland, is the seat of the Soul. Its seed symbol is *Aum* and it is the seat of the Self. On a physical level, it governs the autonomic nervous system and the endocrine glands through the hypothalamic and pituitary glands. On a psychological level, it is the seat of pseudo-soul ['Me'] and Soul ['I'].

The causal plexus of command or *ajna chakra* in the medulla is guiding all other *chakras.* Represented by a two-petaled lotus, this seat of the mind or *antakarana,* works in time and space. Its seed symbol is *ksham* for patience, fortitude and peace. It rules through the mind and therefore controls the sense organs and the organs of action.

In the physical brain, the causal body interacts with the cerebellum and the brain stem. Changes in the causal brain are recorded in the thalamus, the Sun *[or surya]* that influences all the nuclei of the basal ganglia or planets transcribed in Man's brain and spinal cord.

The Universe Transcribed in the Brain and Spinal Cord

The Whole Universe is transcribed as nerve centres within Man's brain and spinal cord. Planetary influence on one can be mathematically calculated from latitude, longitude and one's place and time of birth. These deductions serve as signs of things to nurture or to avoid during one's life. Although one cannot change destiny, the power of Will has the ability to change the authority of Nature or *Prakriti,* through restorative action.

The planetary system acts from various points in the brain and spinal cord. *Surya* [the Sun] works from the thalamus above the pituitary gland. *Chandra* [the Moon] functions from the centre of autonomic control in the hypothalamus. *Mangal* [Mars] is the red nucleus and amygdala is deep in the cerebral hemisphere. *Buddha* [Mercury] works from the subthalamus and *Guru* or Jupiter's influence lie in the globus pallidus. *Shukra* [Venus] works its influence through substantia nigra. The unfavourable influence of *Shani* [Saturn] is through the putamen.

Also, *Rahu* [in the ascending Lunar node in the Head of caudate nucleus] and *Ketu* [the descending Lunar node in the tail of caudate nucleus] effect influential changes in Man's life. To evade the influence of compulsion and impulsion of *Prakriti,* Man must move up. He must rise above the pituitary and endure in the thalamus in meditation. Here the pure energy of Awareness has the ability to merge with the light of Consciousness. Here in the *kutastha,* Man will witness the look, the sound, the feel, and touch, the smell and the taste of Breath of *Brahman.* He becomes one with Universal Intelligence of Christ or *Krishna,* the Son of

God. He is One with both Awareness of Matter or *Prakriti* and Consciousness of the Spirit or *Purusha*.

Here Man experiences the Father of all Creation. He meets with the Son shining as Universal Intelligence. He realizes the Father is born of the Son and the Son is born of the Father. Man also intuitively understands the Son is intrinsic in Matter. It is by Her sanctity the Cosmic Mother – the Holy Spirit – begets the Son to serve humanity in all times and in all climes.

Awareness Flows Outwards

The Brain Recycles itself every six years. The human body undergoes physical changes every twelve years. A person's lifestyle influences these changes. Wrong living habits hinder the mind and intellect's ingenious growth and change. Disease then sets in. The quality of life degenerates. The health of bodily and brain cells falls apart.

When Awareness flows outwards, it is out of ownership and pulls by attachment. Wrenching towards Matter arrests liveliness of the higher *chakras.* Span of Man's ignorance of the Self is a linear measure. The distance away from Awareness and the divine cave is in proportion with extrovertedness engaged in wants. The original essence of the Soul becomes increasingly deluded by the power of *Maya* or illusion. Memories of past *karmas* or actions, habits, inclinations and *raaga-dvesha* [likes and dislikes] domineer Man's personality. *Maya's* inherent qualities, the triune *gunas,* further complicate things. There are six outward expressions of Awareness filtered through unenlightened tendencies or *vasana's* empowered physical and astral bodies:

- *KAMA* or LUST [coccygeal] ... the compelling desire is an action for sense indulgence and is compelled by want.
- *KRODHA* or ANGER [sacral] ... born of frustrated desire and manifest as paroxysms of anger from habits in past births - often parading as righteous-anger.
- *LOBHA* or GREED [lumbar] ... enslaving the ego on whims ingrained in the individual's judgment as likes and dislikes *[raaga-dvesha]* directed at food and taste.

- *MOHA* or ATTACHMENT [dorsal] ... expressed as suppression of evolution of the pseudo-soul or ego, which imagines elusively that it is the Soul with its possessions.
- *MADA* or PRIDE [cervical] ... expressed as arrogance, conceit, haughtiness and passionate behaviour for me and mine.
- *MATSARYA* or JEALOUSY [medullary] ... expressed as private internalised ego dissatisfaction despite material accomplishment.

Thus, Ego-consciousness or the pseudo-soul 'Me', parading as 'I', has six faults, which compel one to forget or move away from one's Self or Soul.

Expanding Awareness through Spiritual Centres

The Physical-Astral Transformation of the vegetative biological body, mind, and intellect is achieved through *Raja Yoga.* The wisdom of liberation and emancipation from almost invulnerable impediments occurs in the fire of meditation. Here, Man personally experiences the Reality behind the mortal body. With this reformation within him, Man is sanctioned with a belief in oneself. He is finally connected with the Cosmic Mother. He learns to heal himself. He gradually shortens the span between his outgoing senses and the divine cave in the brain.

The nervous system is more attached to the divine cave than to any other part of the body. Here, Awareness is concentrated in the thalamus. Consciousness lives more in the brain's vertex. Unknown to unsuspecting scientists, they are together sensed around the pineal gland. Efferent stimuli flow from the brain as sensations and thought reactions. The descent through the spinal cord is charged at the cerebrospinal energy *chakras.* This keeps the self preoccupied with material perceptions. Meditation, on the other hand, centralises the afferent flow of *prana* into the *sushumna* or spinal cord. It first rises towards the medulla and then to the *kutastha* above the pituitary gland. The individualised self lives in this area of the brain. Meditation gives Man the power to withdraw Awareness from body parts and concentrate it to the Centre of Life Force, above the pituitary. For this the *chakra* that enlivens the biological body with each inspiration secretly enlivens Man with every Breath.

But how does life force concentrate here? The first

inspiration or *prana* is the power of God that quickens the brain and divine spiritual centres with Awareness. And how can one be sure? The dawn of Knowledge gives the seeker an immediate, instinctive and intuitive understanding that Man exists because of *prana*. Through meditative practice, Man slowly expands this experience to understand his relationship with the entire Cosmos.

This is true evolution.

A meditative experience of a void is a sign: the seeker is in the *sushumna*. He must now enter the various *chakras* to grow and change further. There is a gap in the *sushumna* at the point of the navel, or near the *manipura chakra*. It is here that some seekers meet a 'hindrance'.

Mounting Awareness achieved during meditation meets an obstacle at this point. Efforts for a resolved meditation may stumble. That is because the three lower centres exert the power of negative polarity or *tamas*. In contrast, the fourth and fifth centres exert the power of positive polarity or *rajas*. The meeting of these polar energies at the thoracic centre and especially at the cervical centre bring meditative efforts towards harmony or *sattva*. Further meditative striving shortens the distance between the coccygeal centre and the medullary centre. Such intuitive meditation is a scientific method that quickens human evolution. This happens by effecting near-immediate changes in the nerve cells of the *chakras* and the human brain.

Lack of inner understanding is the basis of Man's sense of separation and fragmentation from the Cosmic Mother. Once intuitively connected, the seeker automatically abandons old habits, ideas, opinions and likes and dislikes. He begins to love God's Image as the Cosmic Mother and experiences Her in every atom, and in every name and form. He has the inner knowledge that 'All is God' and 'God is All'. He now knows knowledge gained from reading scriptures alone cannot give him the experience of the omnipotent, omniscient and omnipresent Energy he experiences in meditation. It is these personal experiences that motivate Man to devote himself to a Collective Good. It is this that helps tame the Ego.

Chitta

There is a point where *ida* [parasympathetic] and *pingala* [sympathetic] nerve channels join the central channel in the *sushumna* which is around and above the region of the pituitary gland. The channels or *nadis* extend above the pituitary into the hypothalamus, but below the thalamus and across from the pineal gland. This central link is aligned with the *kutastha chaitanya* or the Krishna-Christ Centre, between and behind the two eyebrows.

The *ajna chakra* in the medulla is the 'home' of *chitta* or the multifaceted centre of mood and feeling of mind-intellect-ego, taken together. In its pure state, *chitta* reflects, first, into the visual cortex of the occipital lobe. It then reflects into the *kutastha* as the "spiritual eye" where the figure of Man resonates with the symphony of Om. The image is the same as the one seen with daybreak and intuitively identified in the Cosmic Vision. *Chitta* remains here in the medullary centre. It is the address of 'Me' the pseudo-soul. Here stays the causal or *vasanic* personality. Sage Patanjali describes enlightened *chitta* as the consciousness of 'I', without the impediment of 'Me'. When self-control through meditation has reached this level, 'I' reigns increasingly preeminent. Because 'I' has intellectually understood and intuitively seen who he is, Man recognises the wasteful preference of the five mundane *chakras* that cater to 'Me'.

The first effect of this meeting is that Man stops seeking God in the material world. Secondly he witnesses the Self with each breath triggered by the *kutastha*. Feelings are an overpowering emotion and closeness with God happens – this happens at the same time. The third effect is staying within the *kutastha* as a persevering hermit. Enduring here brings with it a perception of God in all actions.

The fourth result of this experience is a realisation. Man is SEEING the Cosmic Vision, HEARING the Cosmic Sound *AUM* in all its symphonic variations, WATCHING the life force enlivening and transforming the biological body, while FEELING breath. It enters the *kutastha* as fine, near imperceptible vibrations of *Prana* or life force. The existence of the biological body is because of Breath that enlivens the inherent energy of matter.

Transcending the medullary centre or *ajna chakra* by concentrating between the pituitary and the fontanel allows Man to cancel all worldly thought. All the bodily instruments - mind, intellect, ego, senses, and objects of senses - merge, come together and dissolve. The unenlightened *chitta* becomes the enlightened *chitta*. With continued intensity of meditation, Awareness of Nature or *Prakriti* comes over into perceiving Consciousness of Spirit or *Purusha*. After that, the instruments of the body experience only Intuitive Universal Intelligence at the *kutastha*. Man is now free from want, anger, greed, possessiveness, pride or jealousy. In this Self-centred State breathing becomes occasional. Man reaches an almost pulseless state of hibernation.

Steady effort at meditation teaches Man to feel Unity, in every form and diversity. The biological body feels, but with devotion to the Cosmic Soul. Life's ups and downs, joys and pains are felt with perfect composure. The mind's turbulence recedes. Senses begin to service the Universe from the centre of the Self.

Knowledge through Intuition

Everyday existence binds Man to his own narrow individuality. This happens when *Prana* is directed outwards through the senses. This unsettling ambush of his body and mind happens through his bodily sensations and passing thoughts. *Raja Yoga* turns this supposedly ineffective life force inwards. Once directed towards his own Awareness of the Self, *prana* recaptures its natural authority to commission Man with spiritual enthusiasm. All religions of the world prescribe understanding life force, the Holy Spirit that enlivens energy in matter. The seeker then transcends the biological body and the mind. However, Man must first know how to reverse this flow of life force at Will. And this needs knowledge of Science of Meditation. The trajectory to this knowledge is firmly fixed in perception, inference and intuition.

The senses receive provocation from objects and the mind catalogues this inducement as impressions. If the mind stores these imprints haphazardly, it becomes confused and disconnected. If an indiscriminate intellect or *buddhi* absorbs these impressions and codifies them against distinct associations like memory, likes and dislikes, or habits, *buddhi* interprets them. It projects them to the various parts of the brain as packaged knowledge. This is knowledge gained through PERCEPTION.

So, when *buddhi* turns back on itself to chronicle Supreme Knowledge of Truth, it remains imprisoned to its own past association with the senses. *Buddhi* cannot see beyond itself. It cannot see into the pre-sensuous knowledge of Knowing, the blissful state of Being.

Knowledge through INFERENCE, whether through deduction or induction, is also based on distinct past associations of a knowledge base. It is popularly said, 'there is no smoke without fire'. But, *buddhi* cannot go beyond itself to experience the happiness or mystery of the Truth. Therefore, although early efforts at meditation and devotional prayers can silence and even still the restless mind, old habits amassed through previous lives, don't allow Man to penetrate the blissful state.

The only way to know the world is through INTUITION. Here senses and thoughts do not exist. This is where all Knowledge of things and beings and the Laws of Nature are embedded, locked away from Man. The only way to reach its threshold is through self-unfoldment. This allows Man to realise intuitive experience and reach the Truth. The power of intuition is held hostage by the frailties of the human form. The body and mind are subject to physical diseases. These result from identifying with objects and ambitions, indulgence, mental incapacity, laziness, doubt and instability of the mind.

These frailties are inherent as *samskaras* or natural tendencies from previous births. Associating with people and situations that induce such injury regenerates them. Willpower and association with the right people and environments allow the spirit of inquiry to grow. For this the 'right person' is the *guru,* a preceptor of God, who has the ability to wipe out ignorance.

Spiritual awakening erases all the negative qualities of Man. He then lives with an assurance that he is full and self-sufficient. With his intuitive knowledge he succeeds, even in the materialistic world. It is this knowledge that has the ability to silence and still all mental turbulence.

Section II
Scientific Evolution

Transformation and Evolution of Man and Nature

With correct training in Meditation, it is within Man's reach to act, spontaneously, under *Prakriti's* laws. The instinctive ability to *not* make a mistake in thought, speech or action is the orderly direction of Evolution. This competency is embedded in Man's own physical anatomy and physiology.

By studying the inter-neuronal junctions or synapses, one can understand there are silent intervals during the conduction of a nerve impulse. Maharishi Mahesh Yogi calls these inter-neuronal spaces gaps. He says that intercellular spaces between cells in the body are similar to the gaps between *mantric* sounds. These gaps are silent areas where new informational inputs impel transformation in the cells around them.

For instance, the afferent stimulating impulse [input] can be sounds of syllables, verses and *mantras* already present in *Vedic* scriptural literature. Since the neuron is the human body's most evolved cell, such stimuli in and around the neuron lead to the highest grade of makeover stimulus, especially if the seeker is meditating along pathways free of mental restlessness, breath control and sensory extroversion.

A pre-synaptic impulse collapses into the silent gap. A transformed expression emerges at the post-synaptic end. It is the same for the changing neuron. If the gap is aligned and balanced, the emerging expression is in tune with the expected sequence of expression. The next emerging syllable or impulse will undergo the same process of collapse, and a third expression will emerge... and so forth. This continues until the outward expression or efferent action [output] is complete.

Meditative Inputs and Transformed Outputs

AFFERENT input **<O<OO<OOO +ive** EFFEREN output

Transformation in the Synaptic Spaces of Nerve Tracts

For every collapse into a 'gap', a new state arises. In neuronal physiological terms, the impulse collapses into the silence of the next space. The emerging impulse depends on the quality of the pre-synaptic impulse. The inner dynamics of the intercellular and synaptic space gives it an altering value. Each emerging impulse, therefore, has an unambiguous unit value with a *chhandas* excellence. This is the foundation of neuronal metamorphosis and natural adaptation in Man through meditation.

Human behaviour, speech and action follow this flawless system of emergence and collapse. All afferent inputs emerge transformed at the efferent limbs of the nervous system. What emerges depends on what knowledge 'collapsed' for incorporation. Depending on purity and balance of the silent, Self-referring gap, thoughts, decisions, words and actions unfurl themselves. This is an exposition of the unconquerable power of Shakti or Prakriti as the Cosmic Mother. Through such implementation of Man's wants, needs and desires, She preserves order in the whole universe. Nothing is ever wasted. Nothing is ever lost. Through the consummate science of metamorphosis, everything unfolds with perfect precision. The gap's state of equilibrium, where the catalyst collapses, need not be expressed in an overt action. The dynamic of Nothingness can reveal its quality into the space in the nerve synapse. It does that also in the causal neurons of the brain and spinal cord.

Man's memory of new Knowledge is aligned with the memory of Total Nature. This memory is embedded in the DNA molecules of thalamic neurons. This memory, which is part of universal recall upholds and ensures that there is order in Creation. It is etched in the Invisible Causal Body of the Universe. This is the secret of transformation in one single act. It may appear as if occurring in an individual mortal but it resonates into the Universe. This is the Path of Evolution through *sadhana* [spiritual effort] of meditation. Eventually, individual *dhyana-samadhi* or meditation absorption takes the seeker to a state where he is One with Nature.

Within the structural dynamics of Prakriti's Laws, the available Self-correcting mechanism always puts everything back on the highway of Evolution. Mother Nature ensures that She can continue to delight Man and creature alike This pleasure appears as an undisturbed flow of Her expressions.

Mastery over the natural Laws of Nature is available to each one of us. It is where its source lies. It is in the silence of the intercellular and synaptic space. Here lies the *atyantabhava,* the Self-referring competence of pure Awareness. Acting from this level means acting while fixed in silence and stillness of body, mind, intellect and ego or *chitta.* This level, achieved through the Yoga of Meditation, is 'action in non-action'. This leads the seeker to real freedom. Such freedom is also from boundaries imposed by partial and non-Self-referring impulses, including desires that can't find fulfilment.

Wants or *vasanas* are what bring Man to the reincarnation of expression. *Prakriti* offers every opportunity for these *vasanas* to be fulfilled. If the mortal aligns his actions under Her *dharma,* and such actions are virtuous and righteous, there is Harmony. Unrighteous actions to satisfy indulgence create strains in Her creation, both in the microcosm and the macrocosm. Unfulfilled wants also emerge out of tune with Cosmic Symphony, and lead to stress in the Fabric of Creation.

In meditation, all seekers can achieve the state of being One with the Divine Mother. One needn't become a monk or give up caring for relatives while seeking one's own immortality. Many seekers wait till they age to embark on a spiritual journey. Thinking that a spiritual life demands rejection of all worldly wants and family responsibilities, they postpone *sadhana*. This is an uninformed opinion.

The secret of meditation is to begin where the *atyantabhava* or Self-referring awareness presents itself. It becomes master of all transformation, thus guiding one's destiny. This is the Secret of Creation, the Secret of the Creator and the Secret of being One with the Cosmic Mother. No strain, no pain is necessary, ever. A knowledgeable and experienced preceptor is all a seeker needs to reach his destiny of liberation.

The secret to fulfilment of all desire is to act while settled in the Self-referring state of the silent space or gap of pure Awareness. In this *atyantabhava* is a state of complete nonexistence. Man can achieve anything, be anything. He can create gardens out of mud, move mountains and even shake the cosmic structure. But he must be actively resting in the *kutastha*, in meditative stillness and silence. Understanding immortality lies in these same silent, still mechanics of transformation. The complete dynamics of change and evolution are subsets of transformation. There is no impulse of the Self-referring Absolute. It never dies. Every thought, particle and galaxy is transformed. Nothing ever dies. It only becomes something else. The first law of thermodynamics also points to this. Transformation occurs in the silent, unbound, pure level of extreme non-existence. This is immortal in its Self-referring nature.

Every rise and fall in thought [vritti] is a reference to itself. It is the real Self. Each impulse of knowledge, each impulse of Prakriti's Laws is the unconquerable power of Shakti. It is a vibration or pranava of AUM. It is that which supports the universe with Creative Universal Intelligence. Every one of these impulses finds its course in creation, collapse and re-emergence. Thus, the ever-changing field of relativity, cause-and-effect and changing qualities is itself, immortal.

There are two values of immortality in Prakriti or Shakti. One, its own level of Self-referral exists in pure silence [sattva]. And the other is in dynamism [rajas]. In dynamism, the 'act of watching' has no boundaries. One may be fully awake in both states of being the observer and being under observation. Enjoyment of every new possibility or gain and ever-changing experience is all there is. As each impulse collapses, a new experience emerges from it.

Having discovered this, Man must exert oneself to be One with the Universe. He should strive to be in Her silence and in Her dynamism. It is never too late to start, wherever one is. A sadhak or seeker who awakens into this reality can experience the never-ending bliss of Creation, its play and its ever-serene face. Peaceful, fully awake and unbounded by the limitless Self, the seeker emerges as everything. Seeing the glory and joy of creation he is released from the cycles of change. Discovering immortality and the unlimited dignity of life, he rejoices. He is because of the Cosmic Administrator.

Modern Science Recorded in the Ancient Vedas

Vedic Literature enshrines Hindu thought. They were and still are, preserved in a large collection of books written and accounted for by *rishis* of yore. The seers are experienced experts of Truth. These ideals and principles were also, and perhaps some still are, in 'oral' form. Passed on from generation to generation in old Vedic families, they still exist. But it was Sage Vyasa who had the unrivalled vision to compile the entire old cultural, political and scientific material in the four Vedas. Vedic literature dates from over five thousand years. He could foresee, back in that era, the impending age of acquisitiveness through indulgences and loss of ethical values. He envisaged worldliness would alter the very underpinnings of Vedic traditional families. He could foresee the oral practice would eventually be lost.

For the same reasons, two thousand years ago, Patanjali, another Vedic scholar, focused on Man's central nervous system to educate the learned students about the existence of a miniature template of the Universe within Man's body. He would show them the science of all orderliness and where it emerges from Nature.

The Laws of Nature constantly whisper to themselves. They describe the natural laws and record all potential laws through a system of Self-referral within Cosmic Intelligence. Each whisper intonates itself into a series of synchronised hums. Such palpitations are of varying frequency and vibration. The whole universe, thus, is vibrating Infinity, from atoms to galaxies.

The Laws of Nature are all encompassing. They include

physics, chemistry, biology, anatomy, physiology, biophysics, and every law known as well as unknown. The laws governing every individual life are also within their fabric. There is, therefore, order in Nature's infinite diversity. The underlying hum doesn't need anything outside itself to justify the existence of the entire Universe. It is self-sufficient under its Self-referring quality. It has also the ability to transform itself in accordance with the Laws of Nature.

Knowledge has an amazing power to self-organise. The more precise the knowledge, the greater its organising power. Pure Knowledge of the Infinite is transcendent and unmanifest. It combines with the power of Pure Awareness [Prakriti] and Consciousness [Purusha]. It contains all possible interaction of the Laws of Meditation in one unified field of experience.

The Universe is born of the relationships with its own parts. It's a system of energetic that structures its own diversity. Self-interacting, self-sustaining and self-sufficient, these dynamics are independent. So, the Obvious Universe or Intelligent Awareness is created in, and is an expression of, Unmanifest Conscious Intelligence or mahat. The Invisible Spirit [Purusha] and the Visible biological Universe [Prakriti] are interdependent, as One Whole [Purushottama]. Just as Man, both visible and invisible, is one. When Man lives under the Laws of Nature that govern his anatomical, physiological, psychological and intellectual processes, ill-health and irrational behaviour are unheard of.

Man is able to fulfil every ambition or want with the Eternal Mother's support. Yes, She is the Cosmic Homemaker. When a group of people collectively understand and adopt this spiritual lifestyle, they can create a coherent Collective Awareness, which eventually erases stress in the Fabric of Creation. There is a real rise in the standard and quality of living and society progresses to a healthier lifestyle. The group is free of disease, stress, crime and antisocial behaviour.

This intense insight, that order prevails in the Universe,

leads one to definite conclusions. The Self-referring capacity of Unmanifest Intelligence gives the objectified universe its own Self-referring quality, despite multiplicity and diversity. That a connection exists between Unmanifest Intelligence and Manifest Intellect, gives creation and evolution an everlasting order.

Study of scriptural material from childhood, through listening or reading, leads to sequential evolution of the developing central nervous system. The growing child, exposed to the Laws of Virtue or dharma, matures into a perfected sequence of progressive awareness. This nurturing of a child's neuronal physiology becomes, eventually, a habit and a built-in thought. This is also the basis of progressive gains made by seekers during sadhana.

Meditation has the ability to transcend the mundane mind and its mental activity. When the physical, psychological, mental and intellectual sheaths are stilled, Man's awareness settles into its own restful, yet alert, silent state. Man now rests in his own stillness and sees transformation. This happens within the boundaries of his Self-referring State of consciousness. Over time, all stress of the past is erased. With new, exalted creativity, Man becomes orderly and dynamic. This inspires and upholds all his thought, speech and action. What is exciting about this transformation is that every want of the changed central nervous system is upheld. This happens because the Laws of Nature sanction it.

The human physiology as chitta [mind, intellect and ego], which stays in the brain, has the ability to be aware of itself, in structure, thought, and action. Chitta also has the ability to understand and experience itself as the enlightened chitta of pure awareness or Universal Intelligence. This happens in the centre of will. It lies within the forebrain and is fulfilled through the *kutastha*. Here, the spiritual eye reflects brilliantly in the astral thalamus above the pituitary. Here is the microcosmic Sun in the brain's planetary system.

Once this view of awareness is obvious Man understands.

He gains capacity to change the settings of the control systems of body, mind, intellect and ego. These changes are recorded in the memory of the microcosmic Sun, or thalamus. It stimulates the master-glands within the brain, and the sympathetic-parasympathetic channels in the spinal cord.

The master glands, which control the autonomic nervous system and the endocrine glands, release altered neuro-transmitters and neuro-hormones that transform every cell in every sheath of Man. These transmitters, being strictly structured, follow precise principles of change. The change depends on the transformation that's unfolded in silent meditative periods. These transmitters also have a definite matching quantitative value. The quality decides the value that goes into the gaps of the afferent or input arc of the nervous system.

The harmonious experience or samhita has merit. It is harmonisation of three circumstances of awareness. Man is now able to realise an exalted sense of being One with the Whole.

DNA of the Human Cell

Each Human Cell differs in size and structure, depending on its role in the body. Between these cells are spaces or gaps. They contain tissue fluids and many molecules. By allowing communication between like and unlike cells in the body, the body resonates with regularity and accord. The central nervous system within the divine cave acts as the head mechanism. It coordinates all movement to provide equal access to all bodily works.

The nervous system's basic cell is the neuron. Within the neuron's nucleus, is the DNA molecule. It contains all the information that a neuron needs to work as the combined obseiver, observation and observing unit. The *observer* or Purusha or rishi or Spirit is the everlasting witness who merely watches without involving Himself. Changes happen in the centre of awareness as *observations* of Prakriti or devata or portrayal of Matter in the thalamus. She looks at reconstruction buried here by Man's wants. All of Creation is qualitatively registered in the DNA essence of the thalamus, in the causal body.

All changes introduced and recorded in the causal seed crystallise as altered action mediated through the pituitary and hypothalamus glands within the brain and spinal cord. The *observing* now is analogue the *observer* and the *observation.* But how does this happen?

Man triggers a want in the afferent channel to the thalamus. Prakriti yields to Man's will and sends a message through a synaptic gap. The postsynaptic efferent impulse is a transformed message. The directive influences the release of altered neurotransmitters and neurohormones from the hypothalamic-pituitary axis. This altered state leads to the natural adaptation of end-organ cell at all endocrine, body and nerve centres. The changes have a principled or finite or *chhandas* quality. Cells become skilful at eliciting suitable cellular and verbal responses, when Man contacts the world through nerve tracts.

Collections of neuronal processes, with identical activity and direction, travel together in nerve tracts within the spinal cord and as nerves outside the cranium and spinal column. Within the brain, they gather as fascicules, also called the white matter of the brain. Collections of neuronal cells, with similar roles, are the nuclear aggregates of gray matter within the brain and spinal cord. Transmission of messages between nuclear aggregates occurs through nerve bundles, via synapses and synaptic spaces. The experience triggered by these nuclear aggregates in the brain and passed on through nerve tracts may be motor, sensory or autonomic in nature.

But the act of observing has been transformed under the will of the individual. In Creation the will of Humankind launching change is forever transcribed in the DNA of Mother Nature's Causal Seed. Man has the authority to vibrate the world towards peace and harmony.

The Brain and Spinal Cord

The Central Nervous System begins in the embryo as a hollow tube of ectoderm. Its cephalic one-third undergoes more proliferation than the caudal two-thirds. The cephalic end is the future brain, and the caudal two-thirds is the future spinal cord. By the third week, the embryo has already developed three areas of the brain. They are the forebrain or prosencephalon the midbrain or mesencephalon and the hindbrain or the rhombencephalon.

The forebrain changes into the cerebral hemispheres or telencephalon. The diencephalon is composed of the thalamus, the hypothalamus, the pineal and the pituitary gland. The cerebrum is divided into four lobes - frontal, parietal, temporal and occipital. The brain surface is convoluted as gyri of folds and sulci as grooves between them. These have neurons a few millimetres thick and are, histologically, highly distinct from each other. Association fibres interconnect the gyri of all the four lobes. The cerebral hemispheres are themselves connected through the corpus callosum and the anterior commissure.

The dorsal surface of the midbrain or mesencehephalon forms the tectum and has superior and inferior colliculli. The ventral surface or the tegmentum has two cerebral peduncles of large bundles of nerve fibres.

The hindbrain or rhombencephalon changes into the upper metencephalon that becomes the future pons and cerebellum. The lower myeloencephalon narrows and becomes the spinal brain or medulla. Within the core of the brainstem, a collection of nuclei called reticular formation and tracts form a complex and detailed structure, with diverse roles.

Each part of the brain has the ability to work through a whole range of Man's experiences, be it in his waking or asleep state. Man's WAKER reception is of a conscious mortal. His experience is of the four lobes functionally integrated. By sinking through the six layers of neurons of the neocortex or cerebral cortex, Man experiences a unified awareness even when within the deeper parts of the brain.

Deeper than the neocortex is the mesocortex or subconscious DREAM brain. Deeper still lies the limbic cortex, which encircles the whole brainstem and the subcortical structures of Awareness. This is the site of the brain's unconscious DEEP SLEEP, which allows Man to experience a blissful sense of existence.

The Centre of Will lies within the frontal lobe. It coordinates all changes through the thalamus and the hypothalamus. It is here that all autonomic, emotional and motivational transformations take place. The pituitary ensures that suitable willed transmitters are released into the bloodstream. These willed changes are permanently recorded in the thalamus and fulfilled through the thalamus-pituitary-hypothalamus-pineal-medullary axis.

The subcortical structures of the cerebral hemisphere are the deep-lying basal ganglia. From this level of control, human physiology plans and carries out the complex motor roles involved in planning, higher understanding and execution of strategies. The basal ganglia are connected with other motor works, as well as the limbic cortex on the medial side of the temporal lobes. With these connections, the brain is involved in logic, reasoning, understanding, memory, and orientation in space, behavioural patterns, self-discovery and motivation.

The basal ganglia lie within the cerebral cortex and encircle the midbrain. This is also where the thalamus-hypothalamus-pituitary-pineal axis is positioned. The thalamus is connected to the brain through four fibre radiations. They are the frontal or optic sensation, the acoustic sensation, the parietal or cutaneous, muscle, joint sensation, the occipital with nonvisual fibres and the temporal for olfactory, gustatory, emotional sensations. The thalamus is the sensory information centre, broadcasting the state of Man's emotion and awareness to the cerebral cortex. The thalamus is, figuratively, a door between the outer materialistic world and the inner world that waits to fulfil its right of self-discovery.

Man uses the brain's frontal lobe to gather knowledge and view it from his own inner conditioning, logic, understanding and conclusion. For further self-investigation, reflection, discrimination and reasoning Man uses the occipital lobe. When an inquiry is satisfactory, his thoughts are stilled and he thinks effortlessly from the back of the brain. With self-unfoldment through meditation, there is a deeper thinking and a progressive self-discovery and maturity. This sense comes from the insula of the parietal lobe, also known as the Seat of Bliss. If nurtured by an experienced teacher, Man is taken into the limbic cortex of the temporal lobe, where he experiences the synchronised awareness of meditation.

The hypothalamus also plays a major role in autonomic homeostasis towards a physiological equilibrium. It receives input from the limbic system, the thalamus, the cortex and the reticular formation. It augments itself by transforming the stimulus through a feedback system. Regulating motivation and the autonomic nervous system is an important function. It is in the hypothalamus that life force vibrates and the Spirit beams in its Light of Consciousness. The enlivening Energy of Awareness as Prana penetrates it with every in-coming breath. This individual connection infiltrates into the five sheaths and three bodies of the mortal, through the Mouth of God in the medulla. So long as there is life in a mortal, the medulla is connected to the unseen cosmic life force.

The cerebellum wraps the whole midbrain, the pons, and the medulla. It integrates all information from motor and sensory input originating in the cerebral cortex. Through the spinal cord it preserves the balance of the body despite the forces of gravity, through the inner vestibular nerve system.

The brainstem is composed of the midbrain, pons and the medulla. The nuclei of cranial nerves are also embedded in the brainstem. Within its core lies a collection of nuclei called the reticular formation. The brainstem governs sleep-wake cycles and the body's biological rhythms. It must be noted the twelve cranial nerves emerge below the kutastha. The gaze into Cosmic Vision is beyond and above the individualistic mind, the senses and the pituitary.

The spinal cord consists of collections of motor and sensory tracts activating organs of perception, organs of action and of behaviour. Perfect integration of these components' role is achieved by means of feedback loops that exist within the system itself. To ensure instinctive control and balance, the efferent response is multiplied by upholding continuous contact with the source of impulse. The impulse source is the hypothalamic-pituitary complex. For a neuro-physiological impulse to be relayed, an efferent stimulus must be processed at synapses through eight factors. The progressive transformation of this stimulus takes place in the gaps. The integrity and integration of the eight factors within the synapses is perfect.

Each of these eight factors elaborates a particular stimulus estimate. This happens during sadhana or spiritual effort. There is a gradual transformation of the quality of neurotransmitters and neuro-hormones being elaborated from the hypothalamic-pituitary axis. What then is the effect? There is a gradual transformation of eight matter factors in the seeker's seven psychic chakras that are lodged within the divine cave.

- These eight factors are products of Prakriti – they are: EGO or ahamkar, which lives in the medulla.
- INTELLECT or buddhi, with the discriminating quality of clearing channels for onward conduction.

It remains on the hemispheric surface and is connected to deeper structures of the brain.

- MIND or manas, capable of emotion and thoughts. The limbic cortex and complex represent it. The centre of willed transformation in the thalamus is the causal template that influences the quality of *messenger*-transmitters stimulated for *release*-transmitters through the pituitary-hypothalamic axis. These neuro-hormones and neurotransmitters influence the autonomic nervous system and endocrine glands.
- SPACE or akasha, within the synaptic gaps in the autonomic channels, is the cause of specific effect by neuro-hormones and neurotransmitters. It lives in the psychic cervical centre of intuition or vishuddha chakra.
- AIR or vayu exists within the gaps for exchange of gases and is represented by anhaata chakra or the thoracic plexus.
- FIRE or agni exists in the gaps for transmission of impulses, through a feedback system of electrons and electrolytes. It is represented by the manipura chakra or lumbar plexus.
- WATER or jala exists within the gaps for ionic constitution and osmosis along cell membranes. It is represented by svadhisthana chakra or the sacral plexus.
- EARTH or prithvi, gives structure to boundaries between gaps along cell membranes. It is represented by muladhara chakra or the coccygeal plexus.

These eight factors combine, integrate and modulate into the DNA of the neurons of the brain and spinal cord. All the rhythms, cycles, and Laws of Nature and of human physiology are recorded within these molecules.

The basic unit of DNA is a codon. With sixty-four possible permutations that decide the transformation possible in the structure and function of the neuronal cell, it has many potentials. And on this structure depends the neuron's memory bank, of every exposure and action endured through its millions of incarnations. The complete memory of the present existence, for elaboration of a studied action or perception, remains in the surface layers of the cerebral cortex.

Feedback Systems of the Brain

Sensory Nervous System

During his Wakeful Existence, Man experiences his environment or its circumstances through specialised sensory channels. They represent sensory modalities that give Man his observer or *Purusha* or *rishi* status. As the *Purusha,* he merely witnesses and watches from the vertex in the fontanel and the pineal gland.

The perceptual special senses and sensory equipment allow Man to organise, balance and decode all incoming stimuli. These are recorded as observations in his Prakriti or devata. Man wills into Her and the devata [Nature] looks as transformation takes place in the individual within the thalamus. Man reacts by making the necessary adjustment through the hypothalamus and the pituitary gland. The thalamus is also where the psychic third eye is found in the *kutastha,* directly opposite the *ajna* centre in the medulla. The third eye, it is said, is a reflection of the sixth centre.

Man's bodily functions are fulfilled through processing systems. Parts of these Man experiences. Inputs such as eating, drinking and breathing are experienced as offerings of sacrifice or yagna to the body. These are metabolised in the fire of physiological digestion, psychological emotion or feverish thought, depending on the intent of the sacrifice. Any input for excessive indulgence is also metabolised in ways that harm bodily functions. This is because input causes the release of fitting, whether favourable or harmful, precise neurotransmitters and neurohormones from the master organs – the pituitary and hypothalamus. These specific agents enable a reciprocated efferent stimulation. The stimulus may be favourable or harmful.

Every experience of the body is in strict accordance with afferent wants and input. This is the basis of altered actions and relationships with the world after sincere sadhana. All the eight factors of Nature, present in Man, must undergo permanent conformation of change. Sages are of the opinion that it takes at least six years of sincere concerted effort to make visible changes in the seeker's habits, ideas and likes and dislikes embedded in the brain. Physical transformation on the other hand takes twelve years.

Sensory and Autonomic Nervous Systems

There are two categories of processing systems that exist. The *Shukla* or white or somatic system is the first. The second is *Krishna* or black autonomic system that is also called visceral. *Shukla* or sensory and is open to awareness. *Krishna,* which includes the sympathetic or pingala and parasympathetic or ida, is not.

Shukla or somatic input is the conscious experience of the body surface. It knows through fifteen modalities of insight. These are sound, sight, taste, cold, heat, sharp pain, burning pain, light touch, sense of air movement, pressure, vibration, proprioception for limb position, joint capsule sense and the sense of balance. The last three are with reference to a midpoint of the body. *Shukla* sense modalities are channelled and controlled by the hypothalamus, which lies below the thalamus, the centre of Awareness and above the pituitary. The pituitary and hypothalamus are master glands for molecular arrangement of neurotransmitters and neurohormones respectively. The thalamus corresponds to *Surya,* the Sun. Besides influencing the hypothalamus and pituitary gland, the thalamus coordinates all motor and especially sense of the body, as well as every part of the brain.

Krishna or autonomic input is channelled through the autonomic ganglia of the cranial nerves and the sympathetic-parasympathetic systems. It is also controlled by the hypothalamus, the master autonomic ganglion, which also controls emotions in the limbic cortex and the conscious brain. There are four recognisable aspects of the *Krishna* system. These include inhibitory and excitatory modalities of sympathetic and parasympathetic systems that release chemical transmitters. The hypothalamus is associated with *Chandra* [the moon] and guides the parasympathetic or moon-channels or ida. Moon channels unconsciously cater to Man's *tamasic* indulgences, processing input based on Man's intent. The hypothalamus is also involved with the creative or *rajasic* activity of the sympathetic or sun-channels or *pingala.*

Together, these systems respond to the thalamic ability to make changes in the DNA codon. The thalamus makes changes in response to afferent input. The changed message is then relayed to the hypothalamus to release changed neurotransmitters and to the pituitary gland to activate changed neurohormones.

The 'Looks' of Awareness

Man's awareness in his waking state leads to his consciousness of his self and his environment. There are two aspects of wakeful awareness. One is content - the sum of mental functions. And the other is arousal, which is, behaviourally, closely linked to the appearance of wakefulness. Content and arousal work independently. The content of consciousness is assigned to functions of the cerebral hemispheres. Arousal of consciousness is assigned to the brainstem.

Since consciousness can be estimated only by a person's behaviour, its presence, degree or absence is sometimes difficult to judge medically, especially during states of psychic withdrawal in meditation. Wakefulness requires that incoming sensory impulses constantly stimulate the cerebral hemispheres. Fred Plum and Jerome B. Posner have experimentally proved this. They found the cortico-thalamic connections are diffuse. Fibres connect Consciousness from cerebral hemisphere that **watch** with the diencephalon nucleus or the thalamus which **looks** with Awareness.

More important, however, is the mechanism that activates the transfer. The reticular activating system [RAS] consists of ascending fibres from the reticular formation, a collection of nuclei that is at the core of the brainstem. It extends from the midbrain to the diencephalon, with diffuse projections to the cerebral cortex. The main sensory pathway is by means of the thalamus. Anatomically, the RAS has indistinct boundaries and extends along the core of the central brainstem from the lower medulla to the thalamus, incorporating small and large neurons.

In the thalamus, the RAS is interspersed among other

main nuclei. There are close connections to the forebrain, especially with emotional behaviour and memory. It connects with the Dream State of Sleep in Sub-consciousness. The caudal extent of RAS is in the pons and the medulla. It presents as the Deep Sleep State of Unconsciousness.

The thalamus works on the sensory input in the causal template. Through the ajna or medullary centre, it provokes suitable responsiveness in the five senses. It induces extrovert wakefulness and triggers suitable action about objects. In the introvert state of meditation, Man withdraws from all sensory input, while fully aware and conscious within the RAS. This psychic wakeful awareness impels a transformation within every cell in the body. Man experiences changes as the inward journey of *Prana* to every body part. Body consciousness can be felt without the grossness and density of matter that characterises an outward journey.

The other nuclei that form part of the reticular formation control Man's waking, dreaming and sleeping cycles. In the pure aware state of meditation, Man is in the *chitta.* This mind-intellect-ego complex is under the control of the thalamus, the metaphorical Sun or Surya. The ancient seekers of faith call it the spiritual eye, the Krishna or Christ Centre of Universal Intelligence. Man must enter to reach Awareness and merge here with Consciousness. It is the door to Man's connectivity with the Cosmic Mother first and then with the Spirit.

In the *Chitta* State of meditation, the seeker experiences a sense of relief from imprisonment. Preoccupied with his senses, thoughts and desires he remains veiled. The coverings are lifted and truth of past births, once invisible, becomes obvious in his understanding. The seeker intuitively begins to understand where he is and where he is heading.

Action through Motor and Skeletal Systems

Man gets his shape moving capability from the musculo-skeletal system. It also covers the body's inner physiological psychological systems. The body is capable of shrinking and expanding and moving at major joint levels. Man establishes individualistic harmony with his environment, through this mobility and adjustments.

The vertebral column is shaped like a bow. When held taut and firm, it upholds the physiological systems of Man's body. It remains undisturbed, unchanged while supporting the transformations that course through its tunnel, seen as a blue passage in near-death experiences. It is invincible in spite of the assault of a diversity of environment change. It is geared towards maintaining evolutionary balance and perfect order within the universe.

The cavity of the brain and the spinal cord is the divine cave, the altar of God. The spinal cord houses the five chakras or centres of psychic energy in its plexuses. Here, all human physiology rests in silence and dynamism. Old molecules of DNA are constantly destroyed and new ones produced, recording every change in input.

This structure and function have a quality of invincibility. As Man's body obeys the Laws of Karma through action reaction, he lives through *gunas* or qualities of Matter. Through opposing relativity, these unchanging influences are recorded in the causal body. These, eventually, make their effect felt in the bodily enzymes. Man's biochemistry and his immune systems are also affected. It is here that the blueprint of a healthy or diseased bodily state lies, in the present and in bodies yet to come.

The Higher Bodily Pacemakers

Bodily Pacemakers are integral part of the feedback mechanisms of the human physiology. The human nervous system, for instance, orchestrates the body from different levels. The thalamus co-ordinates all sensory and motor input into the brain. The hypothalamus governs the type of neurotransmitters being released. The pituitary gland determines the type of neurohormones that must be released. The limbic system absorbs the effects of these changes. The basal ganglia determine the health of Man's physical structure and the co-ordination of its parts.

The centres of logic, memory, intellect and social behavioural norms lie within the cerebral cortex. The medullary centre of ego brings in *prana*, breathing life into the body's physical-physiological-psychological functions. If devoted to the search of the Self, Man can achieve self control, sense control, heart control, breath control and withdrawal from the five senses.

Non-discriminating Man tends to be miserable. His senses are restless. He is veiled in spiritual darkness *[avidya]*. Lacking self-knowledge he wants what he sees to be his. In this bewilderment, it is difficult for him to overcome biological forces. The extrovert mind, intellect, ego and senses use his bodily pacemakers for indulgence and ambition. Guided by attachment, he pursues vanity and exhibitionism, self-praise, hypocrisy, pride and other negative tendencies. But, through the power of meditation and breath control, he can learn to withdraw from all these tendencies.

Knowledge of these pacemakers can make Man an expert enthusiast. Combined with the guidance of perfect preceptors, Man can turn into an expert at introversion, in both spiritual and worldly matters. He can withdraw towards the *kutastha* or the Centre of Universal Intelligence.

Mere theoretic and words of how to use bodily pacemakers is not knowledge. It must be experienced personally, for only then can Man discriminate between immortality of the Self and the impermanence of the biological body and pleasures of indulgence.

Putting mantras like **ham sa so ham** into contemplative use is powering higher bodily pacemakers for purposes of evolution.

Education

Though School and University education fortifies the use of the mind and intellect, it seldom gives Man an idea of the Self. Man has the creative ability to harness scientific knowledge. He can grasp that Science of Creation is based on particle principle and linear velocity. But he continues to see God outside himself, in far-off Infinity.

Through meditation, Man gains infrequent Intuitive Knowledge. He recognises chitta or his mood personality as an intimate opinion of himself. His ego tries abandoning its feigned authority over environment. He witnesses his biological body becoming a victim of indulgence. Feeling powerless his body decays. He sees physical exercise as a means to self-preservation. He finally realises that indulgence has given him a body incapable of enjoying the fruits of his hard work.

But his blind mind-intellect continues to plod along this slavish path. When real happiness seems elusive and distant, the introspective Man begins serious inquiry. He wants to learn how to silence the mind-intellect and still the body. By studying the yoga of meditation, he can involve himself in the eight injunctions or ashtanga yoga. He learns to move away from plural hysterical mind-set. Belief is the Body-Mind-Intellect has been created to satisfy Man's indulgence. The discovery of meditation is an essential step in the search for the real Truth. Discovery of psychic centres or *chakras* in the divine cave is the first lesson in such education.

Chakras are spiritual energy centres within the divine cave. They are also anatomical neuro-physiological centres controlling almost all the works of the physical body. Starting from the base of the spinal cord, each ascending *chakra* represents the five elements: earth, water, and fire, air and space. Each of these elements has a sensory connection with smell, taste, sight, sound and touch respectively. The yoga of meditation command the Does and Don'ts *[yama* and *niyama]* that regulate Man's desire for indulgence. Its practice involves harnessing the first two *chakras* in the spinal cord. The third ascending *chakra* calls for constant practice of yama and niyama, through control of sensory desire and speech.

The *chakras* natural tendency is to be attracted outwards towards Objects, Emotions and Thoughts [OET]. Man must reverse this flow and shorten the distance between the divine cave of *prana* and energy in the matter particles of objects of desire. Wants are atoms of condensed energy. Objects are vegetative matter atoms attracted to condensed awareness. The space between these atoms and enlivening energy must disappear. This results in transfer of the body's nucleus within the divine cave. Here lies the temple of God with seven doors. To enter the temple, the divine cave must be magnetised with increasing awareness. Thus illumined by the soul, whose presence is obvious with each incoming breath Man transcends the compulsions of want. The mind, if focused below the pituitary, is about dealing with the perishable world. But above the pituitary, it is in the home of the imperishable Soul.

A true seeker of knowledge aims for a search for the Self. This is true Education.

Association Nerve Fibres in the Brain Cortex

The Yoga of Meditation has an unifying quality of self-referring awareness through association fibres in the brain. Despite diversity in thought and physical-psychological affliction, meditation can cover all possible differences. Through this route, Man himself holds the ability to rise above such interference, despite the everyday bombardment of a million physical, physiological, mental and intellectual stimuli.

This integration is a function of the association fibres of the cerebral cortex. These threadlike units are axons of neurons found in the cortical gray matter. Woven into a fine mesh, bundles of U-shaped fibres connect the gyri of the brain surface. Longer fibres pass through the anterior commissure and corpus callosum to connect the right brain to the left. Some yogis are of the opinion there are 196 association fibres that match Patanjali's 196 Yoga Sutras recorded as aphorisms. The right brain has a common refined all-encompassing quality. The left brain is distinctively analytic. The grand scheme of Nature is to connect specificity with generality. It is to create wholeness, a total. Everything, therefore, is interrelated and connected to the whole.

Each side of the adult brain's cerebral cortex is divided into six anatomical layers of cells in the four lobes [frontal, temporal, parietal, and occipital]. This is where all diversity of expression is represented. With meditation, the seeker progressively enters the deepest layers of the brain. Here motor and sensory input ends, in the thalamus.

The first layer of the cerebral cortex receives input from all other layers, but projects nothing. The brain's full potential is realised when Man carries the experience of pure Awareness in all of thought, opinion and action. This is unity in diversity. The brain's cell allows a gradual withdrawal of stimuli for transcendental Self referral. This takes Man to self-sufficiency, autonomy and independence. This happens in a field of increased inner-directionality.

The second layer of neurons stills all unwanted noise from entering awareness. Deeper levels of meditation give Man a greater sense of intimacy and empathy for the Whole, and he senses an all-pervading wholeness. The integration has a quality of complete stillness.

The third layer is connected to nerve bundles and the cortico-cortical fibres and commissures. Widespread integration and processing within this newfound self-referring ability of Man exudes a quality of omnipresence.

The fourth layer connects to the thalamus in the unmanifest state of a sensory experience. Once Man enters the thalamic level, all sensory input is silenced and there is increased emotional stability, friendliness, loyalty, tolerance, respect for others and compassion. This is universal awareness of the unenlightened *chitta* [the mind-intellect-ego complex].

The fifth layer of neurons contains the pyramidal cells of the motor system. With gaining increased intrinsic spirituality, these experience an unfolding of awareness for a known quality. The integrated personality becomes more aware of own relationship with God's omnipresence. This leads to deeper enlightening of the *chitta* and this open-mindedness allows Man to see diversity of a whole. He now realises he can combine the unmanifest parts into the manifest whole. With heightened mental and physical well-being, he develops a greater sense of social responsibility. There is an unfolding of his persona to increased creativity. He may now join to *siddhic* or psychic experiences.

The sixth layer of the cerebral cortex also contains pyramidal cells, where axons extend into the thalamus, dissolving all unwanted input. This is where the integrated activity of the nervous system lies. Here the final stage of dissolution allows a deep state of rest, free of the body's physical and physiological functioning. This is the state of unity of Awareness with Consciousness or *chit.*

In this state, consumption of oxygen and carbon dioxide elimination decrease and tidal volume is reduced. Respiratory rate is lowered and there is periodic breath suspension. Heart rate drops to basal levels and all biochemical, metabolic and hormonal works of the body are suspended to hibernation level.

Memory and Automated Reflexes

Memory or *smriti* exists within the DNA of every cell. It is especially in the neurons of the gray matter of the temporal lobe, the brainstem and the spinal cord. Man's 'perfect automation' is the result of perfect memory at neuronal levels. He is entrenched further by a full range of possible connections throughout the nervous system.

Smriti is represented in all memory-systems and reflex arcs that allow for rapid perception and action without the need for lengthy processing and analysis. An automatic reaction occurs, governed by complete knowledge of correct motor, mental or emotional response, to any given situation. This response is always appropriate to the situation. It can consist of complex adjustments in socio-traditional behaviour, in the presence of changing circumstance or environmental demand.

Memory has the structure of intellect. It displays the observer's or seer or purusha or *rishi's* total potential of the processes of observation, whether at an individual or a universal level. Man's memory has the potential to be incorporated into the memory of universal value. This ensures a spontaneous absorption of all individual action for a holistic value in Nature. This happens especially when such spontaneous responses are under Laws of Nature. There are silent gaps between the interconnecting fibres of the reflex arc. They have the ability to gauge the needed response and have a *prakriti* or *devata* of mouldable quality. Taken from an individualised potential to Cosmic potential, intellect has an ancient, eternal quality of Awareness. Seeing has a structure of the intellect. This is especially with its ability to display the total potential of blossoming human experience.

The total potential of Man's process of observation is found in the Great Intermediate Net of the brain. Here is the centre of Will in the frontal lobe. Connected with the medulla-pituitary-hypothalamus-thalamus axis, it oversees input and output of the central nervous system.

Reflexes provide the correct response. Based on intended action, individual needs and environment demands they are actual response. The Great Intermediate Net of almost 400,000 neurons matches with the 400,000 neurons in the spinal cord. These include all the neurons and their fibres within the nervous system. Reflexes explain the individual potential of human experience. They have the ability to assimilate the Laws of Nature in Man's thought and action. Physiologically, this is represented by neuronal fibres, which activate the musculo-skeletal system that controls action and speech.

Descending and Ascending Tracts of the Central Nervous System

The Spinal Cord is the most ancient part of the central nervous system. It gives expression to all automated channeled actions. The descending tracts of the central nervous system have a *chhandas* value or a specific final quantifiable quality. This is especially obvious in structured speech and action. All the eighteen descending bundles are motor tracts. They shape expressions of behaviour, action and speech.

The fasciculi propria or spiral nerve fibres are divided into six sets of spiral-spinal fibres. They are short, crossed and uncrossed, ascending and descending fibre systems. They begin and end within the spinal cord. All these sets, from various levels, end at similar vertebral and spinal cord levels. They are interconnected within the spinal pathway of individual intrinsic value.

The fasciculi propria are effective whirlpools of activity. They are moving structures for material expression. The stirring quality of spiral-spinal nerve fibres has a *prakriti* value that oversees all changes. These revisions are accepted as observations in awareness. This innate self-referring awareness explains the underlying mechanics of processing and transforming. These are living examples of material expression.

The rising tracts of the central nervous system bring every possible sensory experience to awareness. These sensory pathways channel individual expression to higher cortical centres. Here expression is made out in a holistic value. These pathways include those for sight and sound. They act as channels that make every experience accessible to the cortex, in one symphony of experience.

AYAM ATMA BRAHMA || *All of this is my Self*

A seeker fixed in pure Awareness or *chitta* has the opportunity to expand. Over time, Awareness merges into the experience of pure Consciousness or *chit*. From now on, every experience is realised in terms of the unbounded, infinite and transcendental self-referring soul. The use of the sensory ascending tract is the supreme purpose of every experience in Meditation.Their point values leads to a gradual unfolding expression. These values are an expression of one's own Soul. As he grows in inner understanding, the seeker responds in sequence:

PRAGNYANAM BRAHMAN ||*This awareness is Self*

TAT TWAM AS ||*That also is my own Self*

The use of ascending channels leads to the most refined and crowning of experiences, where all point values are understood simultaneously in the Oneness of Life:

AHAM BRAHMA ASMI ||*This soul and* Cosmic *Soul are One*

These four *mahavakyas* or great-utterances are discussed and elaborated on, in the 14 main Upanishads. There are about 300 significant Upanishads in the four *Vedas* that describe the transcendental experience of Awareness and, eventually, Consciousness. This happens through a process of meditation and is also described by Patanjali in the *Yoga Sutras*. These *mahavakyas* are *upanishadic* declarations. They express the highest vedantic truths about the identity of the individual self with the Self and then Supreme Self. One *mahavakya* is found in each of the four *Vedas*. The first is found in the Aitreya Upanishad in Rig Veda. The second is found in the *Brhadaranyaka Upanishad* in *Yajur Veda*. The third *mahavakya* is recorded in the *Chandogya Upanishad* in *Sama Veda*. The last of the four *mahavakyas* is in the mighty *Mandukya Upanishad* of the *Atharva Veda*.

Reaching the Soul through Breath Control

The restless mind is extrovert and prone to errors against the Soul. Over time, Man realises there is no real happiness in emotion or materialism. Fatigued with his toils, he reaches an experienced preceptor. He or she enlightens Man with the understanding that his daily life is directed from the brain. And although familiar with the existence of his breath or *svas,* Man acquires information about the incoming breath of life force or *Prana* that enlivens his visible and invisible body. He begins to understand that it is the indwelling Soul - ***Sa*** - in the brain, within the invisible body, that draws in *prana* – **So** - to unite and enliven his energised body – ***ham.*** In this manner, soul and Self are united in an act of union or *yoga.* With each cycle of breath of ***ham-sa-so-ham,*** it performs the consecrated work of living.

Normally, Man breaths 18 times and the heart beats 70 times per minute. During deep sleep, when the mind-intellect is at rest, heart and respiratory rates drop to basal level. Breathing or *swasayama* is deep, slow and relaxed. Satisfactory oxygenation through *pranayama* of the brain, heart and lungs it keeps the body alive at a basal level.

Breathing and heart rate are, however, more rapid during stress, apprehension and excitement. Under the *guru's* guidance, Man learns to work *[karma yoga]* for common good. He sees the common thread that binds humanity by understanding world scriptures *[gyana yoga].* Through meditation, he sees the power of worship and love for humanity *[bhakti yoga].* He, then, is freed of mental distraction and restlessness.

Raja Yoga is based on natural respiration. To master the mind, respiration is trained to become restful, well proportioned and soothing by timing it with the *mantra* ***ham-sa - so ham***. Man feels the Self or *sa* or *so* inhaling through the nose and spreading the life force or *prana* to every part of the body or *ham*. An experienced preceptor always teaches him.

Breath or *prana* is the living God in each one of us. Once familiar with divine inhalation, Man sees a new goal of awakening for real happiness. It enables him to live for the highest form of existence. The extrovert mind finds itself charged with the power. He is able to transcend human limits. The mind withdraws into itself. Man is able to realise the Soul's omnipotence.

So long as a mortal stays in the womb, he does not need a separate respiratory pact. During this period, life force or *Prana* moves wordlessly through his spinal cord or *sushumna*. *Prana* and nutrition is pumped into the foetus through the living mother's placenta. After birth, as soon as the breathing process starts, the previously internalised *prana* is exteriorised with the first breath the baby inhales. What follows is a spontaneous triggering of movements of self-propelling respiration. Oxygen in the inspired air enlarges into life force to support Man during its lifetime as a mortal. The infant's life, now, becomes enchanting and externalised.

Whether wise or dull, the foetus is in a deep slumber of delusion. His awakening is at birth. His wakefulness begins with memories of his previous births. As he embraces his new environment, his mind incorporates his past with his new worldly existence. His feelings and worldly ties blossom through infancy, childhood and youth. Now, a new cast - made of the present - encases his memories.

Memory of his divine past going into the present is the journey of life force towards his inner Self. It is Man's *sahaja karma* or natural act towards materialization. It is made possible only by an inward flow of *prana* and achieved by *pranayama* or breathing. This inward direction of *prana*, however, is not permanent. Demonstrative extroverted-ness reverses its usefulness.

Man can reverse the outwardly directed *prana* for materialism. Meditation and breath control is the path and means. A habit of constant practice enables both mind and breath to become serene and placid.

The mind, eventually changes direction on the wings of inward bound *prana.* When both mind and breath are silenced, Man can fix his attention and focus anywhere in his body. He overcomes the temptations of the world. Absorbed in the supra-mental zones above the pituitary, Man experiences true Knowledge. He understands the Truth of his Existence.

The experience of this Reality is like a new Dawn. The Sun unveils the night of ignorance in a splendid vision of a rudimentary daylight. Individuality is like Dawn. It strips Night's existence only when it enfolds the Sun. Meditation awakens Man to a similar personal realisation.

Section III

Instincts

Automatic Reactions Have Roots

Every word Man uses in his daily life has roots. The language he employs reveals what is hidden in his mind's recesses. Their origin is from past experiences and births. Unknown to him, difficult situations in life are processed and remain embedded in his personality. He comes to terms with them through a series of adaptive reactions.

Beginning with self-pity, attempts at striking a blow against actual cruelty, or imagined injustice, is Man's reaction stemming from egoistic sense of self-worth or an imaginary sense of self-importance. Yet, Man should and must, question whether all actions have hidden motives. What part do these motives play in his urge to strike back?

Undesirable characteristics in the garden of the mind must, first be studied and then, weeded out forever. Because the Law of Karma applies to negative, destructive as well to positive thoughts and characteristics, Man must be able to decipher action. Until we look at our ugly tendencies and accept our negative impulses, we can't recognise and appreciate the positive ones. If we postpone the weeding of the garden, we allow it to be overrun with the negative. Procrastination or denial may blot out Man's continued existence and anticipation of a 'next time'. Each of us must ask, Do I know myself? How do I regard my own life?

Physical symptoms and negative thought patterns are, characteristically, individualistic. They shape our lives and experiences through constant repetition. Our childhood centres on core themes. These involve 'being safe', 'getting love', belonging, self-support, the need for validation, 'knowing through understanding', common support, perfection, 'the ability to give love', commitment to community and culture, attention, and 'abandonment' There is also the question of Cosmic connection which needs answering.

Illnesses or well being is linked to our beliefs about us. Our relationships with others and our true kinship with the Universe, as also our past lives influence our present life experiences .The modern family, often called the 'nuclear family', is unstable, socially. It lacks the resources to deal with urban stress. The added baggage of failed ambition, expectations, loneliness and conflicting signals about important matters from all direction makes our worldly transactions worse. This is comparable to how a child feels on the first day that he enters school. He faces what he feels, as he will as an adult. Threats, frustrations, unexpected compulsive behaviour and unresolved issues are a child's reactions. In adults backlash stems from actions endured in infancy.

The devaluation and alienation are issues that lead to victimisation. Learned helplessness, feelings of weakness, inability to control issues or situations are diversions away from the Cosmic Energy, AUM. Negative thought patterns create negative emotions of pride, non-forgiveness, hostility, despair, cruelty and thoughts of self-destruction. All adult experiences must be analysed.

Inherent restlessness and the mind's flow towards extroverted materialism are instinctive responses. These result from a life of duplicity and corruption. Man is neither told that God stays in his body temple, nor does he understand that breath is the power of God. He cannot understand control of breath can change his life. He instinctively utters many forms of speech, both good and bad. He talks of money, emotions, love, service, kindness, cruelty, and hypocrisy... even about the scriptures.

But if Man can be taught to stop talking, he learns to hear the inaudible, formless Self. He masters functioning from the higher centres above the pituitary. Learning to cancel the automated lower and destructive extrovert tendencies he learns meditation. It transforms Man from an automated weakling to a self-confident being.

But Man unconsciously lives in ignorance or *avidya.* Born of flesh, he wants things of the flesh. Scriptures assert the Divine Kingdom is within him and nobody needs to wait for physical death to arrive at Liberation. Meditation promises Liberation here, now... through this perishable body. The path to spirituality is the central nervous system and the destination is the Soul, which lives in the brain.

By meditating in the reflection of medullary centre *[ajna chakra]* and the fontanel in the parietal brain *[sahasrahara chakra],* Man can achieve the divine experience of seeing the elusive but visible illumination of the *kutastha.* By penetrating the glabella above the pituitary and remaining in the *kutastha* without thought distraction, Man can see the indwelling Soul, whose effulgence is like the Sun... and beyond darkness. But without a teacher, one sees only darkness when one closes one's eyes. Darkness is ignorance. Man isn't aware of the indwelling Soul or how to get to it. With the right technique, as taught by a *guru,* and deep need to know, one can learn to make out this self-effulgent Being.

Physical death is the natural passage out from the coils of humanity. It happens with the last breath in exhalation. It is the moment of emancipation from body awareness. It is, truly, an instinctive activity. With consistent meditation and through *pranayama,* one can learn to direct one's life force to touch the *kutastha* and concentrate on the visible self effulgent Being. He allows a final exit through the fontanel.

This same imperishable *pranic* energy, which is One with the effulgent soul, empowers the physical body through astral centres in the medulla and the spinal cord. Through meditation, negative tendencies and biological forces are metamorphosed. This energy draws Man into the *kutastha,* above the pituitary gland where he experiences stillness and silence.

There are two qualities in every human, the divine and the materialistic. The latter part is absorbed in memory, monetary wealth, and pleasure of the senses, addictions, fears, ambitions and indulgences of the mind. Ignorant of true value, distracted at every moment, consumed by new want and fickle by nature, Man hesitates between right and wrong, unable to distinguish between them.

Absorbed in the five lower centres and the extrovert senses, Man's *prana* flows downward. The ego has opinions about everything and imposes its will...in ugly scenes of conflict, sense-rousing art and music, sensuous indulgence and materialistic suggestion. It rejects intelligent thought and indignantly justifies its own thought, be they intelligent or profane. As long as thoughts centre on personal pleasure or gain, the ego judges them right. It wants only the artificially sweetened, yet poisonous untruth, of flattery, and resents voices that speak otherwise, even of valuable wisdom. This leads the intellect to a false sense of self-importance and self-sufficiency. His blind conviction is that Man's deeds or actions have no inherent discipline.

Functioning from the first coccygeal or *muladhara chakra,* Man becomes a slave to greed and material possession. From the second sacral or *svadhisthana chakra,* his sense of touch demands comfort and sexual indulgence, and he becomes subject to moodiness and irritability. Unbridled passions leave the body spent and the mind excitable and restless. From the third lumbar or *manipura chakra,* Man becomes a slave to gluttony, an insatiable sensation because of which the physical body suffers from idleness, lethargy and sleep. These grow into debility, ill health and premature old age. The fourth thoracic or *anhaata chakra* is the heart centre of passion and attachment.

The fifth cervical or *vishuddha chakra* is the centre of intuition. Uncultured, it is the centre of pride and arrogance.

If it is cultured, Man is calm and able to hear the *voice of many waters*; the roar that hums AUM, and gradually becomes more distinct and louder over prolonged meditation. When Man follows Soul Culture, he is able to control his breath, magnetise his spine and transform the air for physical, mental, intellectual and spiritual regeneration and rejuvenation. When awareness is pulled up further towards the sixth medullary centre or *ajna chakra,* Man meets divine illumination. At this level, Man can use his Will and power of concentration to enter the thalamus, where he arrives at constant Awareness in the lap of Nature. The Soul wants to be One with Nature and, over time, arrives at this in *samadhi* of assimilation.

Gaining Victory over Thought

Victory in *sadhana* or spiritual self-effort is achieved through consistency with right thought and action. Practicing *yama* or restraints and *niyama* or adherence to pledges of restraints are the first steps.

YAMA encompasses five types of self-restraining actions:

1. NON-VIOLENCE or *AHIMSA*: for non-injury [mental or physical] to be triumphant Man must be righteous and his actions must have the purity of perfection.
2. TRUTH or *SATYA:* every utterance must be delivered without any deception. If this truth should inflict pain, it should not be uttered unless it is worthwhile to another.
3. NON-STEALING or *ASTEYA:* hiding materials that don't belong to the person, in attitude or in behaviour, is a mental tendency that must be avoided.
4. PHYSICAL SURRENDER TO THE SELF or *BRAHMACHARYA:* detachment from sensual vices and occupying oneself with scholarship and meditation ensures that one sticks to the path of self-restraint and chastity.
5. RENUNCIATION or *APARIGRAHA:* renunciation of materialism and satisfaction with life's minimum needs helps germinate asceticism in the mind.

NIYAMA are five rules that must be practiced and adhered to, for successful breath control or *pranayama* and to silence the extrovert mind's restlessness:

1. CLEANLINESS or *SAUCHA:* both physical and mental purity has to be aspired for. Intake of food must be regulated to breed serenity in *Prana.*
2. CONTENTMENT or *SANTOSH:* self-satisfaction and fullness that gives pleasure irrespective of materialism.
3. ASCETISM or *TAPASYA:* preoccupation with the practice of raising *Prana* through the six spiritual centres, and fixing it in the *ajna* reflection in the *kutastha* through *pranayama.*
4. STUDY OF SCRIPTURAL TEXT or *SVADHYAYA:* asceticism is nurtured through devotion to the practice of *Kriya Yoga* until Man reaches the trance-like call of AUM.
5. TRANSCENDENTAL MEDITATION or *ISHVARA PRANIDHAN:* mingling the self with the Self in devotion, and reverence with every breath.

This is the only way Man can move up the ladder of evolution, raising from instinctive behaviour. Each individual is automatically positioned on the evolutionary spiral of natural evolution. The *sadhak* [seeker] uses a scientific method of meditation for this evolution, and the *yogi* [advanced seeker] wilfully reverses the flow of Awareness from Matter to Spirit. The *yogi* uses the same channels of the brain and spinal cord that were used to lower the Soul into the body to become the individualistic self. The only difference is because he directs the life force from the body to the Cave of Awareness in the brain.

The more adept the *sadhak* becomes, the greater the divine influence of enlightened *chitta* [mind-intellect-ego complex] on him. Delving deeper, the *yogi* develops awakened discrimination. He is able to free himself from egoistic attachments and earthly possessions. He frees himself even from the friends he had for his indulgence and pleasure.

He progressively becomes a renunciant. The motive is

not denial. He undergoes natural expansion towards his Self-inclusiveness. Having achieved his goals in life, his love goes beyond his family and friends or self-centred *[tamasic]* giving. It expands to include love for his community or *rajasic* [larger-circle sharing]. Gradually, he expands to loving Mankind or *sattvic* [expansive sharing of oneself]. Because he has the experience of being One with Nature and Her creatures, he becomes unreserved. None of these gains, however, are automatic, for the *yogi's* actions stem from unconditional love or *prema* for Her as his own Mother.

The human body is a City of Nine Gates - two eyes, two nostrils, two ears, the mouth and the excretory and reproductive openings. Because these Gates are usually open, the mind remains active and restless. This is especially so when Man is turned towards the mundane.

But, except for the nostrils, these Gates are easy to close. In meditation, Man shuts his eyes. Tutored by a teacher, Man is cultured to watch the imperishable divine illumination in the *kutastha.* This needs time and persistent effort until stillness arrives to continue and silence prevails.

By closing his ears, Man hears the divine sound, the *antardhvani.* But if he has arrived at stillness and silence, Man hears the oceanic echo of AUM in every cell of his awareness. By regulating his breath, Man controls the restless mind. But when within the *kutastha,* he is unaware he needs to breathe. He now has the freedom to meditate. With condensed *pranayama,* Man unconsciously closes all Nine Gates. He arrives at a breathless state. He can place his attention above the pituitary and remain there for as long as he wishes. The experience is of a stillness of bliss.

Action and Reaction

Yama and *Niyama* are actions that are the preliminary *musts* to erase negative qualities in the seeker's personality. They avoid the temptations of materialism. *Gurus,* however, say this is not enough. Because the power of *Maya* exerts compulsions through Nature's qualities or *gunas,* Man is tempted to gravitate towards Mother Nature's duress. The seeker needs an inner detachment achieved through right understanding and personal experience. This is wanted to prevent him from falling back into the bondage of his old ways.

Man has ambitions and wishes, which, according to his inborn tendencies or *vasanas,* prompt actions and reactions. That is the Law of *Karma.* Unless action is with a spirit of duty renunciation and detachment or surrender, Man must suffer the fruits of his actions. While focused in the *kutastha,* this is possible. Actions dedicated to the *kutastha* can be renounced and detached from.

The instinctive *me, mine* and *my possessions* is ingrained in Man. He continues to walk through life as if he will live forever. He may, rationally, have understood that death is unavoidable, but Man forgets or chooses to forget. If Man would reclaim the conviction that he must work under the Self-created destiny, he would gradually develop an inner renunciation. With such recuperating renunciation, practiced sacrifice, austerity and charity to work selflessly, leads to relinquishment of action.

The real worker is the breath of life or *prana.* Only with breath can any work happen. Breath flows in because the soul, ***so*** empowers the physical body, ***ham,*** to perform every action. This must be personally experienced through the practice of *Kriya Yoga.* He realises this when Man raises his total mind to the *kutastha.* The mind becomes silent only when the seeker is free of breath-consciousness. He, then, recognises that every action is worship of the soul.

In this state of inner expansion, breath control keeps Man's awareness preoccupied with the self merging with the Self. His ambitions and desires are sublimated into instinctive renunciation of the present and future lives. His breath is sacrificed into the fire of the divine cave in the thalamus, above the pituitary. This act is an offering of the restless mind. It is for a singular thought of the divine. Man practices a permanent austerity to concentrate on the *kutastha.* Here he sees a reflection of the *ajna chakra* in the *kutastha.* This is the centre of Awareness, the centre where God or ***sa – so*** abides as long as there is this life in Man for living, whether he be an introvert or an extrovert.

With every action, the practitioner lives the renunciation and relinquishment. He knows it is ***sa*** that makes ***ham*** transact - whether it be in action or inaction. He, therefore, suffers no reaction. He is, eventually, exrovertedly active, but feverishly inactive inwards.

This is the secret of action. To free him of materialistic ambition, Man's work must be ***worship*** to fulfil the divine will. It then becomes his destiny. For the present, his action must be for self-unfoldment for Self-realisation, through breath control.

Maya, the Power of Illusion

Ambition fuels Man's urges to attachment. Desire fuels his instinct to own. Distaste is his instinctive reaction to any previously experienced pain. Real pleasure is the experience of perfect joy when his self transiently meets the formless Self. Attached to the compulsions of the lower spinal centres, Man breeds pain through ambition, attachment and temptation. He is shackled to *Maya* – Nature's power of illusion and delusion.

Fragmented and separated from Nature *[Prakriti* or *devata],* Man makes the mistake of culturing his instinctive bodily tendencies to own objects, agree to restless emotions and accommodate wandering thought [OET]. If choosing good company would include a spiritual preceptor, Man becomes a nurtured child of the Cosmic Mother. Worthy qualities are necessary for self-unfoldment for Self-realisation. They are gained easily. Adherence to *yama* and *niyama* are pressing qualifications.

But this is not acclaimed. Indeed, many of these qualities are necessary for a spiritual journey. Absence of pride, freedom from hypocrisy, patience, simplicity, love, service of Nature and *guru,* purity, steadfastness, detachment from materialism, composure in birth-death-old age-disease, nonattachment to family and objects, and so on are all necessary. Implicit faith and regular practice of *Kriya Yoga* allow these qualities to blossom in Man. The ability to examine and watch his own thoughts, moods and dispositions also allows Man to progress on this difficult journey. By cultivating these qualities, Man can regulate restless breath and guard himself against negative qualities.

The formless God, who permeates every cell and atom

of the body, empowers the five senses with each breath. But He or She is, forever, compassionately detached from the senses, the organs of action and the objects of indulgence. Although He is obvious in the whole body, His special home is above the pituitary, above and beyond the three *gunas* of *Maya.* Man then transcends the compulsions *Maya* exerts.

In his delusion, Man ignores what is taught and even denies His existence. The ignorant Man cannot sense Him, though He is and in everything. Man has to be taught to feel Him in every breath and action. It is not possible to watch or realise Him *[Purusha* or *rishi]* or *Prakriti* without the help of a realised teacher. The *guru* must have had the experience of both darkness of ignorance and the light of enlightenment in his own divine cave.

Depending on his age and ambition, Man remains preoccupied with extrovert activities. But if he has been nurtured in truth and purity - by his parents and teachers - he knows that he was born for self-unfoldment and Self-realisation. Most try to reach the doorstep of God's temple when overcome by difficulty, disease, worry or anxiety. It is Nature's law that trouble brings Man to Her for *blessings in disguise.* These are times when Man develops a burning need to embark on a spiritual journey. Often the frailties of the physical body make this impossible.

Some are born with a tendency to Soul Culture and Self-realisation. Destiny allows them to meet the perfect teacher. Man has a developed necessary devotion and tenacity to embark on a spiritual journey, through *Kriya Yoga.* The method is purely scientific. The seeker can reach tranquillity within minutes. Through breath control, there is inner transformation. Life force *[prana]* becomes a divine force, spiritually moulding the body, mind and intellect. When this happens, the soul *[sa]* remains in the body *[ham],* enabling Man to break away from *Maya* and Her qualities, as well as his own tendencies.

Spirituality

Spirituality is not the content of scriptures, nor is it analysis by intellectuals. It is an intimate experience. It is realising a true seeker nurtured under the grace and guidance of a realised *guru*. Many say *God is All and All is God.* But, this revelation becomes a personal experience when His glory is revealed in the fire of deep meditation. The seeker can, finally, confirm that He is indeed knowable, even though He is the knower.

When Man aspires to spirituality, he seeks the formless God. His life suddenly begins to radiate with truth, light and true knowledge. He is freed from spiritual ignorance and is settled in truth. Man feels released from the extroverted compulsions of money, materialism, lust, food, drugs, alcohol, possessions, pride and ego. Focusing his attention above the pituitary, he enters the realms of those qualities that nurture Soul Culture. Man was born for self-unfoldment and Self–realisation. But he must awaken the power lying dormant within him and in Creation. His extrovert activities cloud the light of the self and the Self. He needs help to walk through the darkness, into the light.

While on a spiritual journey, Man must change his lifestyle. By nurturing his lifestyle through *yama* and *niyama,* he awakens spiritual qualities, and *Kriya* meditation helps him quicken his evolution. Unless he is focused on reaching the highest goal of liberation *[moksha],* the Self can't unfold in the centres of Awareness and Consciousness. As Man experiences breath and the light of divinity while approaching the *kutastha,* he discovers the foundations of spirituality. Intense practice leads him, by breathlessness and pulselessness, to the discovery of calmness, self-unfoldment and, eventually, Self-realisation.

Spiritual practices must have scriptural sanction. Hidden in the world's scriptures are a few secrets. The indisputable meaning only realised masters unravel. Many seekers reach the doors of such teachers, but remodel commanded techniques, instead of practicing the training. Instead of seeking Soul-emancipation through Soul-unity, many continue to engage in constant battles with the ever-present temptation of materialistic indulgence. This captivating and impelling force drags the Soul away from the Spirit and down towards the lower centres.

Spirituality, in essence, is a *direct* view of the Light and experience of the Truth. According to *Kriya Yoga,* the seeker must enter the divine cave. He then LOOKS at and into the cosmic vision of Awareness in the *kutastha.* He WATCHES as all the shenanigans witness. He HEARS the Cosmic Sound of Aum. He FEELS the breath with exclusive insight that breath is what God is. He smells and tastes the nectar dripping from the back of the throat. His five senses are engrossed and such captivation allows Man to reflect on the self meeting the Self.

The seeker must concentrate on every change as he enters the layers of his body. He must not make any judgment. Releasing all seeds of past beliefs is a precondition. As he reaches the sanctum of stillness and silence, he allows Awareness to encompass him. Once plugged into It, Man experiences perfect happiness. In meditation Man is One with Creation.

Meditate Constantly

The easiest way to manage the continuously restive human mind is to regulate breath and learn meditation. It is instinctive to focus on the sense objects. But the mind can be calmed if Man is taught to see God's presence – in all things, plants, creatures and beings. The mind's calmness has the quality of divinity because the mind can constantly focus on the One and not the Many. The mind becomes what the seeker thinks that God and he are One.

Breath control through *Kriya Yoga* ensures the seeker learns breathlessness. If he practices these *yogic* techniques, he achieves an introverted state during, and even after, meditation. *Kriya Yoga* is the method, but it needs constant practice or *abhyas*. When he climbs the first three lower centres to the upper two centres through meditation, the seeker is consumed by a sense of divine calmness.

Many, however, are unable to uphold this for too long. This is because the material world is not just alluring, but persuasive. Even with regular spiritual practice, many incorrigibly come down to the familiar planes of daily existence. A fortunate few – those who practice and recall His Power with each inspiration – remain attentive to Him. By being alert to each breath, the seeker escapes the instinct that seizes him towards contradictory tendencies.

If the breath flows mainly through the right nostril, the mind is restless and in the *rajasic pingala,* the creative sympathetic nerve channels. If the breath flows mainly through the left nostril, the mind is lazy and in the *tamasic ida* or sluggish parasympathetic nerve channel. When breath flows equally in both nostrils, it is harmonised between the two pulling powers and is *sattvic.* In such a state it is easier to enter *sushumna,* the harmonious spinal cord. Here the mind is calm, silent.

Practicing breath control in tranquillity is associated with unhurried equalised breathing through both nostrils. By bringing the beating into the *sushumna,* the meditating *yogi* easily enters the *kutastha.* On this upward journey of *Prana,* he must go beyond the feeble breath and up to the fontanel in the parietal lobe. Man will go even beyond. In constant unity in the pineal gland, Awareness and Consciousness merge in silence. After reaching this point, there is no separation and no bottom-ward journey ever again.

Every living being obeys the impulses of Nature. But it is possible to go beyond, through constant meditation and leading a strict, disciplined spiritual life. Free from body consciousness and the influences of essence of the gross elements [earth, water, fire, air and space] that dwell in the five lower *chakras,* the body undergoes constant change. If the seeker goes above the pituitary, into the thalamus and penetrates the brain vertex *[sahasrahara chakra],* he can make out the Ancient Eternal Being *[sanatana].*

Stages in Meditation

Engrossed in the Perishable Body Awareness and its compulsive requests, most can't escape *Maya's* illusion and delusion. But a serious student of spirituality can go from Awareness of *Prakriti* to Consciousness of *Purusha* to experience Super-consciousness. It has the quality of combined Awareness and Consciousness. This merging is of Universal Intelligence or *chit* or Super-consciousness. To experience Cosmic Consciousness or *Purushotama* or *Brahman* or God Almighty, Man loses all awareness of his body, mind and intellect. He is beyond and in Awareness and Consciousness. He is in the stratospheric regions of Silence and Stillness. Here he exists in Truth-Knowledge-Bliss. He becomes sat-chit-anand.

The more intense the practice, the more he is able to see the formless purusha *[so]* living in a body *[ham]* with nine doors [eyes, ears, nose, mouth, the excretory, the reproductive]. By constantly watching the breath, he lives in constant truth, purity and virtue. The more the seeker rises to the *kutastha,* behind the two eyebrows and above the pituitary, the more he will transcend *Maya's* power. The plays of Her three qualities *[gunas - tamas* or inertia, *rajas* or restlessness and *sattva* or composure] are compulsive. The seeker transcends the creativity of *rajas.* His subdued breath silences the mind. His thoughts are stilled but in *prana.*

Through deep meditation, he transcends the perishable, physical body *[ham].* The *swasayama* or physical breathing is rehabilitated to *pranayama* or life force breathing. These go with the **A** stage of the vibrating sound **AUM.**

Meditation allows entry into the physiological-mental-intellectual astral body. This energetic body agrees with the **U** stage of **AUM**. This awareness if determinedly guided allows the body to undergo constant change and transformation through self-healing.

Freed from the restlessness of the mind, the seeker climbs above the pituitary to experience peace and joy – the **M** stage of **AUM**. He gains wisdom that is beyond ***ham*** and *Prakriti*. When this wisdom sets in, he loses his ego, because he has reached the pulse-less and breathless stage. The self seeks the Self. Self-unfoldment unfurls itself into Self-realisation. Awareness of *Prakriti* – ***sa*** and Consciousness of *Purusha* – ***so*** are accountable for Man's materialization or ***ham***.

Even while involved in activities of the world, this wise one can intuitively and constantly make out that **A [sa** and **so** or formless *Prakriti* and *Purusha]* activates both the **U** [physiological-psychological or astral body] and **M** [physical body] or ***ham***. By the power of breath God enlivens expressions with life force or *prana*. But it is not easy to reach this stage on your own. The influence of a realised master is important. A burning need to be free is also essential. To ensure the seeker lives in his body focused on what he wants, he needs to live compassionately detached.

The battle of life involves an inner and an outer struggle. Inner battles are against the human weaknesses of virtue and vice, negatives and positives, good tendencies and bad. The outer battles, on the other hand, are against temptations. These compel Man to act on his extrovert comfort with objects, emotions and thoughts [OET]. Man must, constantly, aspire to reach self-perfection, and yes, it is a struggle. But with the grace of a divine master, the battle can be won. For even great sages, such as the Buddha and Jesus, ploughing through spiritual journeys is easier said than done because of the obstinate ego.

Spiritual Progress

The Foundations of Spiritual Progress are inner purity and constant consciousness of Him, through breath awareness. The worship of God as Awareness of *Prakriti* or Nature and Consciousness of *Purusha* or Spirit is taught by all religions. Masters or *gurus* know sages and saints who articulate the same. These wise ones ensure the seeker is on an equitable path. He is led along paths of duty *[karma]*, knowledge *[gyana]*, devotion *[bhakti]* or physical proficiency *[hatha]*. Man with special tendency must be led along passages of his inclination. But, all human inclinations gravitate towards meditation.

While meditating in the Centre of Awareness in the *kutastha,* the seeker can distinguish the Cosmic Vision of the Self shimmering within. It equals the symbol of the Universe. Enclosed within a yellow light energy of the gross body is the astral energy of blue hues belonging to the subtle body. Deeper still lies the reflective essence of the causal body. Deeper still is the Spirit of Consciousness. Man witnesses his breath energized into *prana,* the life force.

The Universe is also filled with *mahaprana*. Man hears space filled with the symphony of *AUM*. He cherishes the Spirit of *Purusha* and the Nature of *Prakriti* in himself. He sees them in every manifest Creation filled with plants, animals, and creatures - in all things.

The illumination he gains in the heat of meditation allows him to transcend his old habits, concepts, tendencies, lusts and wants. As he enters spiritual life in this state of inner purity, with the grace and help of a realised master, the seeker is taught to magnetise the spine. This ensures the transforming inner physiological-psychological *prana* bathes every atom, molecule, cell, tissue and organ to uphold this inner purity.

The seeker, automatically, moves away from the lower spinal *chakras* [centres]. Functioning from the higher *chakras* Man upholds truth, love and intuitive understanding. He learns to regulate the use of his senses and organs of action. He uses them to benefit as many as possible, eventually.

The tongue must be controlled. The six things that bring about the biggest hindrance to Man's evolution are "a haughty eye, a lying tongue, hands that shed innocent blood, feet quick to rush towards evil and bearing false witness with lies" [Proverbs 6:17-19]. Sincere students of *Kriya Yoga* avoid anger, pride and hypocrisy. They have trained themselves to utter the truth without being offensive. Their speech is sweet, truthful, worthwhile and pleasant to the ears and hearts of listeners.

While deeply entrenched in constant awareness by ***sa*** of the breath, Man is filled with consciousness ***so*** that *prana* enlivens the body. The seeker may continue to live and achieve successes in a material world. But he is all the while fixed inwardly in the formless Awareness-Consciousness *[Prakriti-Purusha]*. This is Soul Culture. Association with such like minds is blessedness. They communicate with God.

Mind Control

Thoughts take birth in the right side of the brain, while the left side controls speech. Therefore, to make speech agreeable, truthful, worthwhile and pleasant to others, Man must be careful checking his thoughts. Only inner purity has the ability to harness in both mind and speech.

Learning to regulate and therefore control the breath leads Man towards a spiritual life. It ensures the mind reaches serenity and peace. This state of contentment allows him to live a life of simplicity, silence and self-control. And the best method to discipline restlessness of the mind is to master the technique of breath control *[pranayama]*. The preliminary principles must be adhered to. Whenever a seeker sees he is slipping back into his venerable worldly and outgoing ways, he must restart with *yama* [restraint] and *niyama* [adherence to the beliefs of restraint].

When discontentment becomes ungovernable, Man must relearn to regulate and watch the breath. This silences thoughts. By rolling the tongue in the *kechri mudra* Man learns to control gluttony and verbal diarrhoea. Persistent exercising tames maliciousness and negative tendencies until they die down. This framework of self-control has to be harnessed when Man feels he is falling back to his old ways.

Soul Culture starts with maintenance of purity of body, mind, intellect, thought, speech and, therefore, action. Deeper seekers meditate with a clean body, mind and intellect [BMI]. By fixing their attention in and above the *kutastha,* they endure there until they see the Cosmic Vision. They continue with meditation here until they arrive at a 'dormancy level' of vital structures of the body. Once freed from worldly restlessness, they are absorbed in the formless

Spirit. They persevere until they experience the Universe enshrined in a yellow and blue light.

At this point, they are ready to enter the stage of realisation, true knowledge and wisdom. This is true selfless meditation, with the self-unfolded and near Self-realisation, through breath and thought control.

Self-healing

When a *Yogi* remains suspended in time and space within the astral spinal cord or *sushumna* [during meditation and in breathlessness], degeneration and decay of the physical body is suspended. And his lifetime normally increases accordingly. Assuming that he regulates his lifestyle and obeys the Laws of Nature, he should be able to maintain his physical existence for as long as he wishes, and in conformity with his own will.

Natural physical decay of the body takes place during expiratory respiratory movements. With cessation of breath, the cause of bodily decay is arrested for as long as the *yogi* practices the art of breathlessness.

The art of breathlessness is based on suspension of breath. It is a movement away from the autonomic nervous system channels – parasympathetic or moon channels *[ida]* and sympathetic or sun channels *[pingala]*. When *prana* or life force enters the *sushumna* that is free of the obstructing cross-channelling between the *ida* and *pingala,* it can be channelled directly into the centre of Will near the thalamus-hypothalamus-pituitary complex.

Here, there is no time, any night and no day. There is no death. During deep meditation, when the physical body transiently ceases to exist, as if in hibernation, most of the life force or *prana* concentrates itself within the thalamus in the centre of Awareness – free of the mind, intellect and ego.

Man does not realise, or recall, that when an infant is born, the Cosmic Mother *[Prakriti]* breathes Her own life breath or *prana* into the infant's body. She resides here, and prompts Man to constantly inhale Her power to enliven the energy in biological body as it grows. She, through His power [*Purusha's],* then becomes part of every action, and is the real Doer of every action.

Without the breath, there would be no life and no action. The self is at the base of every action, whether it is by an individualistic or a Self-realised man. Man earns money and chases materialism through the coccygeal or *muladhara* centre. He indulges in his sexual desires through the sacral or *svadhisthana* centre. He enjoys his appetite with the help of gastric fires in the lumbar or *manipura* centre. He displays attachments, cruelty, insincerity, hypocrisy, as well as love and kindness, from the thoracic or *anhaata* centre. Once he has reached the cervical or *vishuddha* centre, he either exhibits pride and arrogance, or has familiarised himself with the ethics of spiritual living... and has developed the power of intuition through meditation and spiritual endeavour.

A *yogi* takes his non-vacillating enlightened *chitta* and life force through the *sushumna* and exits through his astral heart, into the astral heart of the Cosmic Mother. The more Man practices breathlessness, the longer he can learn to live and heal himself.

Kingdoms of Heaven and of Delusion

Both Kingdoms, of Heaven and of Delusion or hell, exist in Man's own body. The body, itself, is divided into the biological *[HAM]* and the spiritual body *[SA* or *SO]*. The soul is ***sa*** or even **so**, *and* pulling by ***sa*** and enlivening with ***so*** the inspiratory breath ensures *prana* is supporting the visible physical body HAM. ***Ham*** is premeditated from Matter. Nature has three inherent tendencies *[gunas] - tamas, rajas* and *sattva.* Creativity or *rajas* is the most prominent of the three. When *rajas* or creativity is inert, Matter displays *tamas.* When inertia and creativity are balanced, Matter is in harmony of *sattva. Guna,* inherent in Matter, is also called *Maya.* It has the power of delusion. It propels Man towards extrovert Matter driven existence.

SA is the invisible, formless Awareness power of *Prakriti,* which is responsible for the first breath in the newborn. **SO** is the power of the Spirit, *Purusha* who exists as the eternal witness in the seventh or *sahasrahara* centre of Consciousness. Both Matter and Spirit are needed for enlivening Matter's energy, with life force or *prana.* It has a symphonic melody of Aum, Hum, Amin or Amen.

The purpose of the *yoga* of meditation is to unite the leave-taking of *Prakriti* from *Purusha.* It seeks to unite the energy of Awareness with the light of Consciousness, in an embrace of calmness. *Raja* or *Kriya Yoga* techniques involve overcoming, scientifically, the extrovert compulsions of the spinal centres or chakras - one by one. Through meditative practices this is possible when taught by an experienced preceptor or *guru.*

Knowing that each inspiratory breath is drawn by the Self and keeps Man's body or *ham* alive is the first step in being alert to the presence of God. At every moment and with each breath Man is taught to be alert because the Breath is God. It is about blending gradually with God-consciousness every minute of Man's existence.

Eventually, this awareness will hasten Man's spiritual journey from consciousness to super-consciousness [Prakriti], to universal consciousness [Purusha] and, finally, to Cosmic consciousness [Purushotama].

By practicing *Kriya Yoga* and focusing at a single point above the pituitary, in the *kutastha,* behind and between the eyebrows Man learns absorption. The flow of breath slows down automatically, but the body continues to live supported by life force. This is the surest way to transform the body, mind, and intellect and drive the self towards Self-consciousness. When the seeker goes deeper into the formless invisible ***sa,*** the breath gets shorter and shorter, until it finally ceases. In this state, there are no bounds of the mind, body sense or ego. There is only a sense of being One.

The great master Swami Hariharananda Giri tirelessly told seekers:

"Breath control is self-control and self-mastery.

Breathlessness is deathlessness."

Breath control renders the mind calm, quiet and thoughtless. Free from disease, it gives Man's lifestyle an essence of purity, humbleness and a sense of alertness. Man develops the power of intuitive understanding. He gains self-discipline through control over the restless, turbulent senses.

The Method and Path of a Spiritual Journey

Man always searches for Infinity outside himself. The power of Energy enclosed in small spaces is greater than all visible expression. All the five senses that absorb or watch cannot fathom it. Infinity is beyond boundaries. By concentrating at the *kutastha,* also called the Krishna-Christ Centre of Universal Intelligence, Man can experience it. The physical Universe is smaller than the subtle Astral Universe. In turn, the Astral Universe is smaller than the Causal Universe. And all three are within the Infinite vastness of God-Consciousness.

The origin of creation is Existence-Knowledge-Bliss, or *Sat-Chit-Anand.* Creation is to coagulate the Bliss of *AUM* into *chitta* [the mind-intellect-ego complex]. As this change into expression, Matter creates divergence and dissimilarity in Time, Space and Distance. With the unveiling of these polarities, a distance is created between the Intellect and the Mind.

The magnetic field of positive polarity is logical thought of Intellect or *buddhi.* The negative polarity of emotions is tied to the five senses, and controlled by the Mind or *manas.* Through the distance, the ego or **Me** sees itself as the Creator.

When these polarities neutralise through repetitive and prolonged meditation, the seeker rests at the fifth cervical spiritual centre of *vishuddha chakra.* Here it innately vibrates with a HUM and Man goes with and into the lap of That Mother.

Meditation, thus, allows the seeker to believe Man is a child of the Cosmic Mother. The seeker's next step is to raise himself to the KSHUM, in the sixth medullary or *ajna* centre. When *hum* and *kshum* become One, **Me** and **I** becom **One**. Functionally divided *prana [pranaya, apanaya, vyanaya, udanaya* and *samanaya*] become a neutral life force. It now emerges as the Infinite *Prana* – the Holy Spirit. Beyond all instinctive action, Man asks when the realisation of this state strikes him:

How can a fish be thirsty?

How can Man ever complain of being tired?

How can the Infinite ask to become Infinity?

Section IV

Scientific Energisation of the Biological Body

Yoga

Yoga, on the one hand, insists that life needs to be watched especially when it interacts with personal and societal rules. On the other, *yoga* warns you against inflexibility in rigorousness of *tapas* that leads to self-mortification. It tells you that every being is divine. Yet it cautions you against the influence of keeping wrong company. The early rituals of *yoga* make exercise a self-engrossing science. As you advance, there is a constant reminder that you're not the body, mind or intellect. Diversity in statements, such as these, must be understood about *yoga* being a science of harmony. Steadiness is achieved through perseverance and not overexertion. The seeker must use discrimination and choose exercises wisely. Yes, enthusiasm is commendable but overexertion may lead the physically unsteady to injury. The path to Truth must serve you, the seeker and practitioner. The company you choose should further your journey to the Infinite.

Physical pain protects the practitioner from further bodily harm. To uphold mental and physical equilibrium, in the early stages, the energising exercises should be gradual, disciplined and balanced. *Yoga* can, then, prevent stress of the sympathetic nervous system or *pingala* and over-protectiveness of the parasympathetic nervous system or *ida. Yoga,* when correctly practiced, becomes a principle of self-regulation.

Modern practitioners of *yoga* have found the human body to be a fascinating study aimed at solving physical, mental and intellectual problems. This understanding has led to emerging exercises that optimise the body's use through conscious participation. With the correct alignment of the body with breath's *Prana* and by directing attention and will towards *yogic* movements, Man sees changes in the body, for the better.

That spiritualism is a serious business reserved only for the aged preparing for their unavoidable death is a huge myth. *Yoga* is a science permeated with joy and happiness *[ananda]*. Whether *Kriya Yoga* is practiced alone or in a group, the self-fulfilling pleasure gained can heal and energise the body. Healing exercises performed by harnessing the Will remove the harmful effects of hypertension, coronary artery disease, asthma and arthritis on the body.

There are healing exercises and there are energising exercises. Both are necessary. *Healing exercises* reverse damages from energy depletion; and *energising exercises* rejuvenate by enlivening decaying cells of the body.

Healing Exercises for Transformation

Healing exercises made fashionable in India and the world over by Swami Ramadev are not his private concepts. They have encompassed humankind as long as the *Vedas* have been. He teaches efficient Breathing Exercises or *Swasayama* for the purposes of effective *pranayama* for the many sites of self-healing. Thousands use them in this twenty-first century. Swami Ramadev spreads *pranayama* through seven levels which together lead to tranquillity of the body, mind and intellect. The exercises are self-healing if done correctly with abdomen in and back erect. They together prepare Man for deep meditation after.

- *Pranayama* using the mantra *Ham Sa So Ham* for five minutes with abdomen pulled in and back erect stabilises the total lung capacity as well as the central nervous system.
- *Kapalabhati pranayama* is forceful expiration through the nose using diaphragmatic muscles for blowing out respiratory air. This is performed for five to ten minutes. The exercise heightens beauty, lessens hypertension and compulsive tendencies.
- *Kapalabhati pranayama* is a modification of the above – audible expiration is sensed in the throat. Forceful abdominal muscle contractions for five to ten minutes encourage movement of residual air in the lungs. Bowel functions are normalised.
- *Bahi pranayama* is performed three times at first and then increased to twenty. Here *apana* is madc to enter *prana* and *prana* is made to enter *apana* with every breath. The perineum and abdominal

muscles are pulled upward with inspiration and held for a few seconds. The neck is flexed forward at the same time. With expiration, the neck is straightened, and the abdominal and perineal muscles are relaxed. With this *pranayama* urinary-rectal incontinence is controlled and hernias recede.

- *Anulom-vilom pranayama* is for equalising the *ida-pingala* nerve channels. The swami recommends they be done for five minutes. Their favourable effects are seen in varicose veins and in joint pains.
- *Brahmri pranayama* is the chanting of nasal Om while doing the Jyoti mudra.
- *Gyana mudra* is the chanting of Om up along the spine, starting at the tail and rising to the fontanel.

Once tranquil in body, mind, intellect and breathing Man is encouraged to stay still and silent and watch his breath while concentrating at the *kutastha*.

Energising Exercises for Transformation

Paramahansa Yogananda of the Self-Realisation Fellowship has described forty-one recharging and energising exercises for the human body's twelve muscle groups. These exercises are aimed at recharging every part of the body's cosmic energy with life force or *prana*. The term *energising* describes purposeful or wilful infusion and diffusion of the enlivening *prana* to and from parts of the body, which allows Man to have conscious management ability over this life force. The individualised source of all *prana* is the divine cave of the brain and spinal cord, including the mouth of God in the medulla. These exercises align the physical body's health with the efforts made in *yoga*. Based on breathing, these exercises also help preserve this alignment and help in its use for a healthy lifestyle. Breath or *prana* is the link between the body *[ham]* and the Self *[Sa or So]*. *Prana* is also the umbilical cord that connects Man with the Universe. It gives Man a continuous enlivening of energy for physical and physiological rejuvenation.

These exercises should be performed with focused attention and willpower. The seeker must strive to gradually transform the physical body, from the cells of his fingertips to, finally, reaching the Core of his being. It can take about twelve years of intense meditation to energise and transform each cell of the body.

- Stand straight, with feet slightly apart, and the weight of the body on the heels and outer pads of the feet. Your arms should be at your side. With eyes closed, try to focus on the centre of Will, in the *kutastha* behind the glabella, between and behind the eyebrows. This is a reflection of the medullary or *ajna chakra* that spreads *prana* to all parts of the body through the spinal centres, the cranial nerves and the nerve channels.

- Pull in your abdomen with chest pulled forward. Inhale slowly, taking a slow full breath through the nostrils, filling your lungs. As you inhale, raise both arms as high as you comfortably can. Then breathe out slowly, until you feel comfortable, lowering both arms to your side.
- Repeat this breathing exercise, this time with diaphragmatic emphasis. Inhale slowly through the nostrils and fill your chest and abdominal cavity. Breathe out slowly, letting out a third of the breath from the abdomen, but holding the *storage volume* in the lungs. You should feel your sternum and clavicle lift, and your chest should feel full, despite exhalation.

  [The diaphragm is the chief breathing muscle of the body. Although we get the impression the lungs fill up and empty out with each breathing cycle, some air - called storage breath - is retained in the lungs after each full exhalation. The amount of air retained in the lungs and the ability to retain this volume determines a person's health. To ensure it is diaphragmatic breathing, contract the abdominal muscles at all times.]
- Don't attempt to straighten the curves of the upper spine by pulling the scapulae forward [slumping] or backward for so-called good posture - it causes stiffness and rigidity in the neck, the shoulder girdles and the armpits. Let filling happen by diaphragmatic breathing and fill your body with *pranic* energy, from head to toe. Once you are familiar with full diaphragmatic breathing, you can sense *prana* filling every inch of the body, without cramping or any tension in any part of the body.
- Now, with eyes closed, raise your inner gaze up, and

look into the Cosmic Vision above the eyes, in the *kutastha* behind and in between the two eyebrows, above the pituitary gland. Roll back your tongue into the soft palate to touch the uvula. This is called *kechri mudra.*

- Feel the inspiratory breath being drawn, naturally and spontaneously, by the power of *Sa* to the residence of the Soul in the pituitary-pineal-hypothalamus-thalamus region of the brain. Mentally chant *[ham]* with inspiration, and then rest as you acknowledge the power *[sa]* enlivening the biological body. With the next natural movement, mentally chant *[so]* and rest in *[ham],* until the next spontaneous inspiration starts.
- Continue until the mind's turbulence subsides with the rhythm of breathing. You will start to hear the Cosmic Sound of *AUM* in its entire symphony. Over time, you will hear, see, feel and immerse yourself, completely, into the exercises that follow.

In the initial stages, the seeker observes contraction and relaxation in each of the twelve body parts:

- feet, calves and thighs
- four sections of the back – perineum with buttocks, lumbar, thoracic and neck
- lower abdomen, front chest
- hands, forearms, upper arms, shoulders, front neck and head

Although Swami Yogananda described his scientific exercises in the early part of the twentieth century, many teachers of *Kriya Yoga* have extensively used, and continue to use, their own variations.

Recharging Exercises for Parts of the Body

With these exercises one can rejuvenate every part of the body with cosmic energy or *prana*, and look to generate a continuous flow of energy for meditation.

A. To Invoke the Divine Cave

- Eyes closed, face the East and focus on the Cosmic Vision between the eyebrows, rolling back your tongue. Try to 'feel' the divine cave in the brain and spinal cord. [This 'awareness' comes over time, because Man is rarely attentive to his spine.]
- Lower your chin to the sternal notch on the chest, and relax, then tense, your neck. This motion awakens you to the spine and to this body part.
- Place your hands behind the neck, and interlock your fingers. Mentally, will *prana* to move from the medulla at the base of the neck to the *kutastha*, and down the spine. Try to visualise a burst of awareness in the cave.
- Feel the Self [behind the glabella] inhale the breath, and distribute it wherever necessary in the body *[Ham]*.
- Remain attentive to the movement of breath in *[ham sa]* and out *[so ham]* of the chest, with a continuous inner chant of **'HAM..SA..SO..HAM'**.
- Start with full-lung breathing for 5 minutes, then move to diaphragmatic breathing for 5 minutes, and then try to direct the breath towards the glabella.

As you progress in meditation, you will feel the breath localise itself in the thoracic to medullary centres in the spinal cord. The rate and duration of inspiration – rest-expiration-rest *[puraka-kumbhaka–rechaka-kumbhaka]* – will self-regulate itself and the respiratory rate per minute will, gradually, fall. The physical, visible respiration is also replaced by internalised finer *pranic* respiration, with time and effort.

B. Relaxing Body Parts into the Divine Cave

1. Recharging all Body Parts

- Stand with feet slightly apart and your weight on the heels and outer pads of your feet. Look Eastwards between the eyebrows at the Cosmic Vision behind the glabella, with your tongue rolled back. Watch the breath until you can feel that mental turbulence has eased.
- With slow inspiration, gently tense [contract] each part and hold, till you have used all twelve body parts:
  - left foot/toes right foot/toes
  - left calf right calf
  - left thigh right thigh
  - perineum/buttocks sacral back lumbar back cervical back
  - left abdomen right abdomen
  - left chest right chest
  - left hand/fingers right hand/fingers left forearm right forearm
  - left upper arm/shoulder right upper arm/ shoulder left neck right neck
  - back and front of head face.
- Hold the contraction tension for about 5 to 10 seconds, while listening to the Cosmic Sound AUM.

- Now, expire [exhale] slowly, and relax the body parts in reverse order:
  - head, jaw, neck fist, forearm, upper arm, shoulder and drop arm, chest, abdomen, back, from top to bottom hips, thighs, calves, feet ... finally, bend your knees
- Repeat this 3 times, with increasing contraction pressure. Watch the breath during expiration.
- Will the body parts to reach into the divine cave for rejuvenation with each contraction, and mentally 'recognise' this power with each relaxation. Ensure your eyes are raised towards the glabella and the tongue is rolled back. This exercise recharges the twelve body parts with the energy or prana AUM.You should try to mentally direct prana from the body parts to the divine cave, and back.

2. *Recharging the Legs*

- With your weight on the left leg [on the heel and outer part of the foot], lift your right leg off the ground.
- Start with flexion of the hip and knee, tighten the thigh, the calf, the foot, while the knee is bent at 90°. Hold the tension for 5 seconds.
- Relax the foot, the calf, the thigh, the hip, while still in the bent knee-hip position.
- Increase pressure in the flexed right leg: the hip, the thigh, the calf, the foot, and stretch the leg out.
- Now, relax the leg in reverse: the foot, the calf, the thigh, the hip, and relax briefly. Repeat 3 times.
- Rotate the ankle, first clockwise and then anticlockwise, 3 times either way.
- *Repeat this range of motion for the left leg.*

3. Tense and Relax Individual Body Parts

- Stand with your weight on the left leg.
- Tense and relax two body parts each, beginning with the right side, and repeat each motion 3 times. Start with the right foot and right hand, the right calf and right forearm, the right thigh and right upper arm, the right hip and right shoulder.
- Do the same range for left side, this time with your weight on the right leg. Repeat 3 times.
- Now, put your weight on both legs [on the heels and outer parts of the feet].
- Briefly tense both feet and hands, and then relax. Repeat this 3 times.
- Tense and relax the body group, and repeat each motion 3 times. Start with both calves and forearms both thighs and upper arms, the hips and both shoulders.

4. Recharging the Chest and Lower Back

- Stand with your weight on the left leg.
- Tense the left chest, abdomen and lower back, as if you are draining into the divine cave. Repeat this 3 times.
- *Do the same motion for the right side, with your weight on right leg, and repeat 3 times.*

5. Shoulder Recharging

- Before starting the exercise, focus your attention on the hands that start the movements – this will help relax shoulder muscles and make movements easier.
- Rotate your shoulders 5 times, first clockwise and then anticlockwise.
- *[Remember, first, the shoulder girdle is made up of the clavicle, scapula and upper humerus. It is connected to the*

skeleton only at the sternum, through the clavicle. The entire shoulder girdle is a free-floating muscular part, which allows for extensive flexibility and movement. Second, the shoulder joint comprises the humeral head joining the underside of the scapula. Therefore, the joint itself rarely causes shoulder pain. Limitation and pain during shoulder movements is because of hunching or jamming the scapulae into the thoracic vertebrae, with 'very erect' posture.]

6. *Recharging the Back*

- Mentally divide the back into four parts, the lowest behind the pubis, the middle behind the abdomen at the umbilicus, the upper behind the chest and the highest behind the neck.
- The idea is to tense and relax these parts, with closed eyes focusing on the East, ears surrendered to the Cosmic Sound and the tongue rolled back into the buccal cavity.
- Tense, and then relax, the lowest part by pulling up the pelvic muscle and contracting the buttocks, first the left side and then the right.
- For the middle part, tense the lumbar region, first the left and then the right side.
- For the upper, pull your shoulder blades backwards, starting with the left side and then moving to the right.
- For the highest part of the back, first tense the left side of neck and then the right.
- Repeat each of these 3 times.
- *To release back stress, do diaphragmatic breathing.*
- *[To improve flexibility of the entire spine, lie on your back, with knees bent and your feet pressed to the side of a chair. Your hands should be on your side. Now, lift your buttocks off the ground, until your back is arched. Hold for a few*

seconds and slowly return to the starting position. Repeat this 3 times]

7. *Recharging the Throat*

   - Without raising your chin, tense the immediate front, left and right sides of the neck for 3 seconds. You will experience a feeling of inner movement beginning at the front of the neck and moving into the cervical spine.
   - Then relax your neck for 3 seconds.
   - Repeat this 3 times.
   - Touch the front of the throat with the healing fingers of both hands, and tense your throat muscles. You will feel Awareness flowing, like the beam of laser. This will recharge the neck glands, the oropharynx and the neck spine.
   - Relax, and repeat this 3 times.

8. *Recharging the Neck [forward+backward]*

   - Drop head down to chest and tense your neck muscles slowly, move the head backward [with neck muscles tense]. Relax, and repeat this exercise 3 times.

9. *Recharging the Neck [lateral motion]*

   - Increase tension in the neck, and move your chin towards the left shoulder, and relax in this position.
   - Again increase neck tension, and move your chin back to the centre, and relax.
   - Repeat this motion, this time towards the right shoulder, and repeat this exercise 5 times on either side.

10. *Recharging the Neck [360 °rotation]*

    - Increase tension in the neck and rotate it slowly – first clockwise and then anticlockwise. Repeat it

3 times either way. Gradually, increase this to about 12 times either way.

11. Shoulder Sway

- Stand with your feet apart [at shoulder-length] and planted firmly on the ground [weight on heels and outer feet]. Lock your knees and relax your torso.
- Rest your hands on the respective shoulders, and swing your body 180°, clockwise and anticlockwise. The head should swing with the body, following its line.

  Repeat this motion 5 times on either side.

12. Recharging the Waist

- Stand with your feet apart at shoulder-length, resting your weight on the heels and outer feet.
- Your legs should be straight and the spine, tense.
- Place your hands at the waist.
- Rotate your torso, starting from the left, but do not move your hips. Only the area above the waist should rotate, and the spine must be tensely straight.
- Rotate 6 times in each direction.

13. Waiting the Spinal Twist

- Divide the spine's divine cave into two – below, and above the waist or manipura chakra (the solar plexus).
- Close your eyes and focus towards the East.
- Stand on your left leg and raise your arms, your elbows bent and fists clenched. Swing to the right, so your upper torso is pivoting at the waist. Remember that only your torso above the waist is

twisting, in the direction opposite to the leg your are standing on.

- Follow the same motion for the other side, and do 6 to 8 repetitions on each side.

14. *Recharging the Spine & Spinal Adjustment*

[Recharge with hands and fingers]

- Stand with your feet apart, at shoulder-length. Roll back your tongue and look to the East.
- Place your hands on the lower back, with thumbs out. Bend your trunk backwards slightly, while pushing your abdomen forward. Arch your back and rise at the heels.
- Push the vertebrae forward and backward with the tips of your fingers and palms.
- Do the same for the lumbar, the thoracic and the neck.

15. *Head Knowk*

[For sensing the vibrations of the inner divine cave]

- Briskly knock your entire skull with your knuckles. Concentrate on each rap and try to feel the stimulation, as your brain cells awaken.

  [Watch for improvement in your memory]

16. *Scalp Massage*

[clockwise+anticlockwise]

- Move your fingertips gently along the scalp, in a rotary motion. This simulates circulation of blood in the scalp.

  [Remember that your fingertips have healing power]

17. *Recharging the Head and Neck*

[Through fingertip massage]

- Press down and rotate your fingertips in small circles,

clockwise and then anticlockwise, along the forehead -> the eyes -> the nose -> cheeks -> the chin -> the front of the neck -> around the ear -> back of the head and neck.

18. *Recharging the Biceps*

- Position your eyes [close, looking to the East], tongue v[rolled back] and focus into the divine cave.
- Place both palms on your head, and interlock fingers.
- Tense, and relax right and left biceps, alternately.

  [You are using the power of Will – in the kutastha – to recharge and rejuvenate the body parts, by dipping into the divine cave]

19. *Recharging the Triceps*

- Position yourself as in the previous exercise, bend your arms at the elbows behind your head, and interlock fingers.
- Tense and relax your shoulders and triceps.

  [Watch-Look-Listen-Feel the life force moving in and out of the muscle group and the divine cave]

C. Recharging with Prana from the Divine Cave to Parts of the Body

This group of exercises is a reversal of previous set. While those directed energy from the body parts to the divine cave, this group transports energy from the divine cave to the body parts. But first, one has to learn to concentrate on the life force [also called *Prana,* Cosmic Energy, AUM and breath] within the divine cave.

- Breathe naturally, merely watching, aware of breath entering and exiting from the body.
- Mentally chant 'HAM SA SO HAM', regardless of

whether breath is going in or out with each breathing cycle.

- *[If breath flows in or out of the body with a burst or out of tempo, always wait till breath flows naturally again.*
- *The purpose of this is to practice breath, so the intervals between inspiration and expiration lengthen naturally, when there is no movement of breath.]*
- With the mental chant 'HAM', breath enters with natural inspiration, but doesn't immediately exit. Wait, and enjoy this momentary breathless pause, and mentally chant 'SA'.
- When the breath flows out again, mentally chant 'SO' with the expiration. Again, wait in this momentary state of breathlessness and mentally chant 'HAM'.
- When breath flows in naturally again, mentally chant 'HAM' once more. You have completed the cycle once.
- Repeat this cycle for about 15 minutes, and try to extend the period ensuring your eyes are focused at the *kutastha* behind the glabella, at the centre of Will. Also ensure that you have rolled back your tongue.
- *[DO NOT willfully regulate your breath to any definite rhythm. Allow the mental chant 'HAM SA SO HAM' to follow the natural flow of breath.*
- *Concentrate on the intervals during which there is no movement of air in or out of the lungs. Watching the breath and resting during intervals convinces the ego that it is the soul 'SA', that breathes and keeps the physical body 'HAM'.*
- *Watching prana calms breathing and quietens the mind]*

With slower rhythmic breathing, muscular activities of the heart, diaphragm and the lungs also slow down, quiet down. The life force now recedes into the spinal cord and becomes available to nourish the cells of the body. In the physical sense, Red blood cells have a longer period for oxygenation and detoxification during these intervals of breathlessness. At this point, while watching the breath, the seeker should personally experience that 'Man does not live on bread [Breath] alone' but with the 'word' of God [AUM], or His power [Prana].

20. The Divine Cave as a Centred Organ

[Extended arms and double exhale with 'huh-huhhh']

- Extend arms laterally while inhaling, and tense hands, forearms and upper arms for 3 seconds.
- Relax from the limit of arms at the fingers as if draining yourself into the divine cave. At the same time, double exhale with a 'huh-huhhh', and feel the energy from every part of the body collapsing into cave. Feel the divine cave as a centred organ.
- At the end of exhalation, bend your knees.
- *[The purpose is to feel the energy in every part of body first emerge and then retreat to the divine cave.*
- *Watch-Look-Feel-Listen while in the divine cave, with your tongue rolled back during the energising exercises]*

21. Recharging the Whole Body with Life Force from the Divine Cave

- Mentally direct life force from the divine cave, as you tense every body part with inhalation. Contract the body parts in a wave. Always start clockwise with the left foot, and end anticlockwise.

  The order should be:

  left foot right foot –

  left calf right calf –

  left thigh right thigh –

  left buttock right buttock –

left lumbar back right lumbar or lower back [behind umbilicus] –

left midback or thoracic back right thoracic back –

left cervical back right cervical back –

left lower abdomen, right lower abdomen [pulling it towards the umbilicus] –

left chest right chest [pulling the chest wall and its contents into the thoracic spine] –

left hand right hand –

left forearm right forearm –

left upper arm right upper arm –

raise arms above the head as you tense left shoulder, right shoulder, front neck, the face, the head.

- *[Always look towards the Cosmic Vision in the kutastha, willing the body parts to rejuvenate. Roll back your tongue.]*
- *Watch-Look-Feel-Listen the tense body parts filling with life force from the divine cave.*
- *Watch your breath and rest naturally between breaths*
- Relax body parts in reverse, starting with the head, face, neck and ending with the arms, lowering them to your side, with exhalation and withdrawal into the cave.
- Complete the motion of relaxation as you double exhale. Finish with flexing both legs.

22. *Recharging Body Quarters from the Cave*

- Mentally position yourself in the divine cave and the centre of will in the *kutastha*, while watching the breath.
- Tense the limb quarters, starting with the lower left limb up to the waist. The focus should be on infusing

energy from thc divinc cavc into that particular body part.

- Clench that part to a bearable maximum [until you experience some discomfort], while all other parts are relaxed. Listen to the inner Cosmic Sound until body awareness recedes into Awareness in the divine cave.
- *[Note that Awareness is the same in the relaxed three-quarters of the body, as in the quarter that undergoes induced pain]*
- Follow the same motion for the right lower quarter, left upper quarter, including the head and neck right upper quarter of the body.
- *[At end of each contraction and relaxation, Watch-Look-Listen – Feel the divine cave, until you feel you are One with the Cosmic Sound. About prana, you personally experience there is no pain or pleasure, no past or present, neither likes nor dislikes. AUM is everything, within and without the different sheaths of human expression]*

23. Recharging Individual Body Parts from the Divine Cave

- Tense, and then relax, each of the twelve body parts, starting with the left foot. Feel the body infused with inspired life current [SA] from the divine cave with each contraction. With each relaxation, feel the energy being sent back to the divine cave.

24. Recharging the Arms

[Bent at the elbows, laterally]

- Clench fists and tense arms, while bending arms at the elbows and, simultaneously, infusing energy from the divine cave to the arms. Breathe in while tensing or withdrawing energy from the divine cave.

- Relax while arms are still at shoulder level, and extend arms laterally, feeling *prana* return to the cave. Breathe out as you relax your arms.
- *[Watch-Look-Listen-Feel while you feel prana inside the divine cave, during the exercise]*

25. *Recharging the Arms*

[Laterally, with *prana* from the divine cave]

- With arms at the side, clench fists and tense arms.
- Hold the tension and lift arms laterally, as if lifting a barbell or weight. Breathe in as you lift your arms, feeling the infusion of *prana* from the divine cave.
- Return the arms to the side, breathing out. Feel energy returning to the divine cave.
- Re-clench the full arm [both left and right] while at the side of the body and rise to shoulder level.
- Repeat this exercise 3 times.
- *[The purpose is to raise both arms up and down to shoulder level, aiding infusion and withdrawal of prana]*

26. *Recharging the Arms*

[In circles, with *prana* from the divine cave]

- Raise your arms straight out laterally, with palms up. Rotate your arms backwards, tracing 3 small circles. Then, rotate your arms forwards, again tracing 3 small circles.
- Now, trace 3 medium-sized circles, backward and forward. Finally, trace 3 large circles in either direction.
- Tense your arms, feeling a recharge of *prana* from the divine cave. Then, relax your arms, returning them to the side, feeling energy return to the divine cave.
- Repeat this exercise 3 times.

27. *Recharging the Fingers*

- Raise your arms to shoulder level, with palms up.
- Tense, and then relax, all ringers with awareness of energy coming forth from the divine cave.
- Rotate your wrists, before relaxing your arms.
- Repeat this 3 times.

28. *Recharging the Arms in Four Parts*

- Clench fists and tense your arms, lifting them over your head. Relax, and return your arms to your shoulders.
- Tighten your fists, forearms, upper arms and shoulders, and stretch your arms out laterally, as if pushing forcefully, infused with *prana* from the cave. Relax, and return your arms to your shoulders.
- Tense your arms and stretch them out in front of you, as if pushing something away. Relax, and return your arms to your shoulders.
- Tense your arms while at the side and flex your arms at the elbows, as if lifting weight off the floor. Relax, and bring your arms back to the side of the body.
- *[Breathe in when tensing the body part and breathe out while relaxing that part.*
- *Continue to be attentive to the power of will while infusing the body parts with prana from the divine cave.*
- *Continue to Watch-Look-Listen-Feel the divine cave]*

29. *Recharging the Arms*

[Up+Down]

- Extend arms laterally. Tense your left arm and direct life force to it as you raise it. At the same time, lower your right arm to the side of the body. Essentially, one arm is going up and the other, down.

- Follow the same motion for the right arm.
- Repeat these motions 3 times.

30. Lateral Stretching, with Breath

- Stand with your feet together, legs firmly planted.
- With your right arm at the side, raise your clenched left arm above the shoulder. Move this arm, with the left chest and left waist, to the right, as much as comfortable. Inhale as you dip to the right. Relax, and return to the upright position with exhalation.
- Follow the same for the right, and repeat 3 times each.

31. Spot Walking

- Focus into the divine cave, behind the eyebrows in the *kutastha,* above the pituitary. Roll back your tongue.
- Stand on both legs with feet turned outwards, the body's weight on the heels and outer pads of the feet.
- Lean backwards slightly.
- Lift the left foot and place it down, heel-first, a step ahead, without taking the weight off the back leg. Just as the leading foot touches the ground, shift the weight to the front foot, simultaneously lifting the back foot, and placing it down, again heel-down.
- Move along the soles of the feet, stepping in a manner the weight is on the outside of the feet. As you develop a rhythm in a slow-motion walk, you'll experience that leaning backwards moves your attention to the leading foot, not the body. Remember to lift the leg at the hips, without straining the knees or the ankles.
- Watch progressive movements of awareness, as you walk with arms and legs swinging alternately. Bend

your elbows and flex your knees slightly, so the weight remains on outside the feet.

- Continue walking briskly for 5 to 10 minutes and note the changes in Awareness, as you enter the deeper sheaths of bodily expression. Watch-Look-Listen-Feel Awareness moving inwards from the physical body.
- *[Watch breath -> Look at Cosmic Vision ->Listen to Cosmic Sound ->Feel the changes, with the tongue rolled back.*
- *Gradually, the body becomes lighter during this exercise, entering within the astral body. It also becomes progressively weightless while concentrated above the pituitary]*

32. *Spot Running*

- Uphold the position of eyes and tongue, picturing the divine cave, as in Spot Walking
- Try to bring the heel up to the buttocks with each stride, and run on heels and sides of the feet with elbows flexed. Follow concentration as in Spot Walking [No XXXI], and run for 5 to 10 minutes or more.

33. *Fencing*

- Bend your arms at the elbows and bring your fists to your chest. Inhale, tense your left leg and step forward.
- Extend the right leg backwards, the foot flat on the ground and simultaneously, clench the right arm and extend it straight out, while double exhaling.
- As you return to the upright position, double exhale.
- Stretch one arm back and the other out in the front, and allow the life force to fill your body, from toe to head. Exhale condensing life force back into divine cave.

- Finally, double exhale.
- Repeat this exercise 3 to 5 times for each side.

34. *Double Breathing, with Arms Raised*

- Double exhale, until all air is expelled from the lungs.
- Extend arms laterally [relaxed] from the shoulders, with hands open, palms up and fingers extended. Hold your breath for as long as is comfortable.
- Inhale twice, taking in as much breath as possible without straining, and simultaneously bend your arms and bring your hands to your shoulders. Again, hold the breath for as long as you can without strain. Feel the tranquillity, and DO NOT tense any body part in this exercise.
- Repeat this exercise 5 to 10 times.

35. *Recharging the Stomach*

- Stand with your feet apart at shoulder-length, and bend your knees slightly.
- Move your trunk forward, keeping the spine straight and place your hands on the upper thighs near the abdomen, resting the weight of the torso.
- Double exhale and without inhaling, pull in the abdomen upwards – towards the chest. Then, force the abdomen and stomach gently outwards, taking in a breath as is necessary.
- Double exhale and repeat this 5 to 10 times. Between each motion, breathe normally and watch the breath.

36. *Recharging the Whole Body*

[With Double Breathing. Follow the path of Recharging All Body Parts No I and practice this exercise in bed, before getting up in the morning]

- With eyes focused at the East and tongue rolled back, listen to the inner sound of AUM.
- Inhale deeply – one short and one long breath – and exert increasing tension in all body parts, from toe to head.
- Feel the energy radiate from the cave to the body parts.
- Exhale in two breaths – one short and the other long 'Huh ... huhh' and simultaneously relax, from head to toes. Feel *prana* coursing through your entire body and then condense into the divine cave.

37. *Recharging the Legs*

[With double breathing. Follow Recharging the Legs No II for its movements and structure]

- Double exhale and double inhale, focused at the centre of will behind the glabella.
- Stand with your weight on the left foot, and lift your right leg off the ground. Follow the movements of Recharging the Legs [No II] and feel *prana* infusing this body part, moving from the divine cave. Follow the motion for the right leg, and repeat the exercise 3 times for each.

38. *Rotation of Leg in a Large Circle*

- Stand with your weight on left leg.
- Lift your right leg and rotate in the largest circle possible. Repeat the motion for the right leg.
- Repeat this exercise 3 times for each leg.

39. *Living without Breath*

- Exhale twice to empty the chest completely.
- View the divine cave and with tongue rolled back, extend arms laterally. Inhale twice as you bend the arms and flex them at the shoulders, without

tension. After that, exhale. Rest between inhalation and exhalation [without any breath] and enjoy the calmness.

40. Reducing Height

[With arms raised]

- Focus your gaze on the divine cave, with your tongue rolled back and watch the breath.
- Raise your arms and inhale.
- Bend your knees, reducing height progressively until the body vibrates. Hold for 3 to 5 seconds.
- Relax, exhaling as you stand up.

41. Reducing Height

[With palms on the lower back]

- Place your palms on the lowest part of back, with the thumbs facing forward.
- Reduce height until the body vibrates, and hold for 3 to 5 seconds. Stand up, relax and feel the changes.

Pranayama

Pranayama is the breathing for enlivening with life force as opposed to *swasayama,* which is the physical act of breathing. *Pranayama* is holding *inspired* and *expired* air and diverting its natural movement by controlling one's breath, as prescribed by a *guru.* The *Bhagavad Gita* describes the technique as oblation of *prana* [up-going life force] into *apana* [downgoing life force] and *apana* into *prana.* The upward-moving inspiratory air *[prana]* rests in the thoracic centre *[anhaata chakra].* The downward-moving expiratory air *[apana]* rests in the coccygeal centre *[muladhara chakra].* The two centres are at opposite poles of the spinal canal. The coccygeal controls negative polarity and is directed away from the brain. The thoracic centre has positive polarity and doesn't normally attract *apana.*

Prana and *apana* are fine in-house energy movements. They support the coarser movements of respiration [inspiration and expiration], visible as chest movements. When *prana* is overcome by attracting *apana,* the soul leaves the physical body. When a *kriya yogi* is taught to scientifically resist both upward and downward movements of respiration, the process is called *pranayama.* Through *pranayama,* when *prana* from the head-to-thorax in the *ida,* and *apana* from the thorax-to-pelvis in the *pingala* reach equilibrium in the *sushumna* opposite the umbilicus, breath settles in the throat-to-head area. This is a state that curbs the movements of *prana* and *apana.* Meditation is then made easier.

Pranayama is made up of three activities: inhalation *[puraka],* arrest *[kumbhaka]* and exhalation *[rechaka].* Inhalation or *puraka* is air retention and is under the control of the cool moon channel or *ida.* Exhalation or *rechaka* is air expulsion and under the control of the warm/solar channel or *pingala*. During *kumbhaka,* there's a spontaneous, momentary pause in respiratory movement when air moves neither in nor out. Scriptures advise holding air in *kumbhaka* at the end of inhalation and exhalation, to reach equilibrium or *samaana*. This equilibrium is experienced in the *sushumna* [spinal cord] when the mind and life force are restfully static. The longer the interval of *kumbhaka,* the greater the meltdown of mind, intellect and ego. This is the foundation of advanced *Kriya Yoga,* and from here on, the seeker learns that life force can be promoted in stages towards the sixth centre or *ajna chakra*.

Kechri Mudra

Mudra means a position that gives Man a sense of pleasure.

Kechri mudra is the retroversion or folding of the tongue within the buccal cavity, to touch the soft palate at the roof of the mouth [at the uvula], while the seeker's attention is on the *kutastha* behind the two eyebrows.

This *mudra* is essential to all the exercises that have been described, as well as those that'll follow. Those who can habituate themselves to *kechri mudra* will not be tormented by hunger or thirst.

When deep in meditation and in this *mudra* for a long time, the *sahasrahara* chakra [the fontanel or seventh centre at the brain's vertex] releases waves of energy. They bring unhindered pleasure, as well as equilibrium in the works of the heart and lungs. When the breath is harnessed, so is the mind. Man experiences the pleasure of his spiritual practice.

Maha Mudra

This posture, *maha mudra,* consists of three phases, each aimed at upholding *kumbhaka* [arresting of breath] and recitation of AUM, while sheltered by the *kechri mudra.*

The practice of *maha mudra* brings pleasure to the five sheaths of Man. It equilibrates air in the lungs, that is, both sides of the chest. *Prana* is directed towards the *sushumna.* There is acceleration of physical, mental and spiritual evolution. With it comes Man's eventual transformation.

The result of *maha mudra* is the spine's curvature and the vertebrae are aligned, in equilibrium. The spinal cavity is freed of osteoporotic collapses that weaken the back by encroaching on spinal nerves. This *mudra* allows the body to resist unnecessary decay as it ages.

Through phases of *kumbhaka,* life force is lodged into the spinal cord and lifted to the sixth centre above the pituitary, into the *kutastha.* Drenching the mind with pleasure and equilibrium, this *mudra,* eventually, heightens spiritual evolution and inner tranquillity.

The Breath

Man's activities and attitudes are so dependent on breath that any change in breath affects them instantaneously. But, to regulate his daily life, Man needs to control his breath. On an average, Man breathes 18 times a minute, or 120 times an hour, or 2480 times a day. When breath rises through the central spinal cord channel in the *sushumna,* Man's breath is short and restful. However, if the breath flows in through the sympathetic or right-sided *pingala,* it is long and restless, because Man is similarly involved in restless activity. When the breath flows in from the left-sided parasympathetic or *ida* nerve channel, it is indolent and slow-moving.

If Man can be aware of every inspiration, he is One with Consciousness every second of every day. And while immersed in Consciousness, Man realises that he is gradually withdrawing from his senses and his extremities. He is moving away from the gross biological body and entering the subtle [astral] body. While interchanging awareness through the astral body, he watches himself becoming buoyant. His body awareness retreats and he is within the boundaries of the astral divine cave.

Man has to learn to protect himself and overcome the impact of his bodily manifestation's *rajasic* and *tamasic* qualities and their compulsions on daily life. Man has to understand that he is multiplicity as well as unity.

He sees multiplicity through the veil of *maya* or illusion. He sees unity in meditation. It happens when breath enlivens the body from above – from the *kutastha.* He intuitively understands that *prana,* which enlivens his physical and astral body, empowers everything with life – be it plant, creature or element.

He accepts his incorporation into the power with his first inhalation at birth. When he concentrates on the *kutastha* and above, he experiences, first, the power of formless God in every breath. Then he lapses into pure bliss *[ananda]* of breathlessness. The physical breath may be suspended but he is upheld by *prana.*

In the words of Swami Hariharananda: 'Achieve breath control. Breath control is self-control. Breath understanding is self-mastery. And the breathless state is the deathless state. This is the highest spirituality.' He urges Man to constantly fix his attention in the *kutastha* and above, to develop an awareness of the real Breath of Life. Man's only *work*, which he must do, is watch inspiring breath, and to be constantly aware of its power. There are fifty types of breath, it is said. But of them, forty-nine are restless, in tandem with extrovert agitation. Only one breath is tranquil, short, introverted... and Man must learn to know it.

This endeavour must be constant and intensely focused, for Man has to realise, through personal experience. He must know the Self and self are One. That is the purpose of human birth. That breath is spontaneous, without self effort. He must come to the awareness that each breath is witnessed until he senses *prana* upholding life.

Waiting and watching patiently within the divine cave and with a spirit of detachment, Man can be sure the Self will come into view. It happens without the hindrances of Nature's triple qualities. Strong determination at regular meditation frees Man from ambition, desire and craving. It frees him from the dualities of pleasure and pain, loss and gain, friend and foe, and so forth. He detaches himself from the temptation of materialistic enchantments. He is neither foolish, nor is he losing his mind. He has come to understand the tendencies *[vasanas]* and compulsions of qualities of matter *[gunas: tamas* or inertia, *rajas* or activity and *sattva* or harmony] in the worldly man, but remains detached.

The constant ability to dip into Infinite Knowledge gives Man the opportunity to make a quantum leap into His Infinite Power. Whether walking, working, speaking or sleeping, he remains focused on the grace of the divine cave. He is able to explain, to himself, his own Eternity.

Naad Shravan

Meditating slowly and deeply, Man spontaneously hears the divine vibration AUM welling from the depths of his heart or *anhaata chakra.* It is as if arising from space and targeted into the inner ear. This is *naad,* the divine resonance of AUM.

When mind and intellect stop their restive activity, Man can adhere to tranquil ecstasy. Man's sense of duality, an innate trait, dissolves. As he moves on to understand, the Self and self are One, his intuition sharpens. His sense of fragmentation away from Nature shrivels. He grows towards unification. His sense of duality from Her transforms into an embrace of belonging to Nature. Man has made the cosmic connection.

Now when *prana* from the *kutastha* reaches the fontanel Man knows success is the character of his journey. The Spirit of Consciousness in the *sahasrahara chakra* embraces the energy of Awareness in the *ajna chakra* reflecting in the *kutastha.* He surrenders the identity of the self into the Self to the tune of the *naad shravan.* Man now has the divine possibility to becoming both Universal Intelligence and Supreme Consciousness of *Brahman.*

Jyoti Mudra

The position that allows one to view the Light of Consciousness, from where Creation emanates, is *jyoti mudra.* Divine Light stays in the *kutastha* opposite the medullary or *ajna chakra.* The quintessence of mind and intellect eases into the Light-Energy, while in meditation. The more the mind ends in its own dissolution, the more visible the Light becomes.

The technique of *jyoti mudra* embraces *kechri mudra* and *pranayama* as well. By closing ears to hear *naad shabda* of Om and with semi-closed eyes focusing in the *kutastha,* Man performs *pranayama.* Earlier while following the divine yellow-white Light, the quality of *rajas* predominates and the restless mind is aware of the external world. He becomes unaware after added concentration. This state of absorption is so captivating the seeker is often tempted to pause here before stopping altogether.

But, with further attentiveness, the strength of Light energy increases. The mind's restlessness subsides and one loses one's individuality with the world. This is the second step. The mind is silent and Man hears symphonies of AUM emanating in waves. He sees the yellowish white Light getting brighter.

The seeker, at this point, is ready to witness the third step. An inner brilliant blue reflection of astral energy or *prana* is now surrounded by the yellow light, shines and reflects in awareness beginning in the *kutastha.* This is the Third Eye of Wisdom normally existing above the pituitary. The eye looks more luminous than many suns, inside its depth lies the final journey through a five-pointed star.

The *kutastha* is the Cosmic Being evident clearly to the meditating Man – in the rising sun from the horizon, the Cosmic Eye re-enacts the cooperation of matter and spirit every day. To recognise this vision mankind needs an experienced teacher to show the path and the way.

Once discovered within, it is easy to make the Cosmic Connection between the Universal and Cosmic Being. Having reached 'home' there is no more need to aspire.

The materialistic world must be walked away from. The path and footsteps had to tread through the forest of the *ida* [parasympathetic channel] and the *pingala* [sympathetic channel].

Once the 'walk' is harmonised, the breath flows through the *sushumna* along the path and steps of *sattva*. A concentrating seeker takes the third step. He enters the inner eye at the *kutastha*. He dissolves into his natural destiny of tranquillity. Besides hearing the divine vibration AUM, he eventually enters that all-engulfing, formless and infinite Light.

Raja Yoga is Kriya Yoga

With each breath meditate, continually. And with each breath, silence the mind. The *yoga* of meditation starts with a *pranaam,* a ritualistic act of homage to the Master or a deity or God. This is the first step towards introversion. The *maha mudra* is a further act of introversion towards the spinal cord and into the divine cave. Introduction into *kriya* is by added introversion and ascension above the *ajna chakra* of the medulla. *Kriya Yoga* is unison of these three acts in meditation.

Given the best way to ease the mind's restlessness is through breath control, one must practice watching the Infinite in ***kri*** in every action and ***ya*** in every breath. Those who practice *Kriya Yoga* learn, over time, and know, forever, how to encourage this godly perception. Even a novice at *Kriya Yoga* can climb to this level. Just as even a rusty wire, if plugged into an electrical socket, is charged with electricity, Man is stimulated similarly. Absorbed in Awareness ***[sa],*** the Self as Consciousness ***[so]*** witnesses body matter ***[ham]*** as One with Creation.

Man gradually becomes what he thinks he is. Just as the river merges with the ocean, becoming the ocean, Man becomes That too. Those who choose to or prefer to remain within the Soul with each inspiration **[sa],** become the soul **[so].** By accepting the energy submerged physical-psychological-astral body **[ham]** as enlivened by the bountiful life-force *prana,* Man is able to detach from worldliness.

Through meditation, Man sees Awareness as a continuous unison of the microcosm with macrocosm. He sees his own individual self in every living plant and creature as built into the Cosmic Form of God. And instead of being attached to the body temple *[ham],* he learns to attach himself and his life to the indwelling spirit *[sa* or *so].* His is true Knowledge born of Meditation.

Nature or *Prakriti,* by Herself, has no existence. The Light of *Purusha* enlivens the Mother Nature's energy with *prana.* Similarly, the physical body can't work without the Soul. The Self, though everywhere, is especially prominent in Man. The human being is able to recollect him as the Universal Intelligence, which comes from the embrace of *purusha* and *prakriti. Sa* entwines with *So* to become That after whom Man aspires in the human body *[ham].* This provides Renunciation from worldliness born of Knowledge.

By practicing *Kriya Yoga* with one's attention above the pituitary in the *kutastha,* one can watch the imperishable soul *[Sa-So],* despite being seated in a perishable body *[ham].* With consistency, one learns to live constantly above the eyebrows. To watch constantly the incoming breath all the time, the body or *ham,* of twenty-four elements, eases restlessness in thought, word and deed. This provides Tranquillity born of Renunciation.

There are four stages to learning *Kriya Yoga.* The first *kriya* is about *dhyana or* study and reflection or Meditation. The second *kriya* is about Knowledge and wisdom or *gyana* gained through Meditation. The third *kriya* is about Renunciation or *tyaga* born of true knowledge regarding worldliness. And the fourth *kriya* is for serenity or Tranquillity or *shanti* and contentment, which give Man steadiness to practice the eight-fold steps of *Kriya Yoga.* Every seeker has the ability to attain each of these four stages. Man must cherish, respect, have devotion and cooperate with his *guru.* All this happens while practicing *Kriya Yoga* to harness *prana.*

Changes in the Brain during Concentration

The Brain is in a constant state of motion and stimulation because of excitement in the five senses. The eyes, for one, carry some form of action in the visual cortex of the occipital lobe. The sensory receptor area from here triggers the perceptual area in the psychomotor temporal lobe. Here the disarrayed sensory stimulation becomes a semi-arranged sensory opinion. This is now relayed into the frontal lobe for determination and confirmation as insight.

Each of the sensory afferent cortexes of the outer brain, depending on receptivity, has an innate rate of excitability. This is seen and confirmed in the electroencephalogram [EEG], a record of the brain's electrical activity. This medley of liveliness makes it difficult for Man to concentrate.

The immobility of *asana* or posture in meditation reduces this physical-mental excitability on the brain surface. This continues until the whole brain assumes a single harmonious pattern of coordinated stimulation. It does this by dipping deeper into the six layers of cerebral cortical cells. Man now approaches the centre of Awareness in the thalamus and remains here until he merges into the *kutastha*. Next he embraces Awareness with Consciousness in the fontanel *[sahasrahara chakra]*. Man does that while immersed into the depth of brain tissue of the pineal gland.

In Man's waking state, the EEG shows alternating sequences of alpha and beta waves, the alpha wave frequency being 9 waves per second. As Man enters a combined state of *dharana* or concentration, with *pranayama* or regulation of breathing, concentrating becomes deeper. He spontaneously sheds his senses in *pratyahara* as he enters deeper into his subtle being of energy. Deeper still he progresses into *dhyana* or meditation.

Alpha frequency recorded on the EEG drops to around 6 waves per second. Simultaneously, alternating *beta* waves become much slower. And *theta* waves now also appear. Deeper concentration cause local synchronised stimulation from the brainstem around super-consciousness. In this state, the sense of the ego's individuality is lost. Man is now left with, in the words of Swami Chinmayananda, a 'quiet, alert and vigilant mind', a precondition to spirituality. At this level, the EEG loses its periodicity and is replaced by continuous *alpha* waves.

The same principle applies to meditation in groups. Their EEG results in synchronised, narrow or group-focused consciousness, with the inherent ability to address the group's action. Countless *yogis,* in fact, occupy Himalayan caves to identify their oneness with the Cosmic Spirit. They nurture humanity today and for eons by invoking benevolence and dedication for all in Creation.

Transformation through Natural Living

From Infancy to Death, Man's life clearly consists of activities that match his granted tendencies or *vasanas*. The *gunas* of Nature that linger in the six lower *chakras* force Man to operate under these general inclinations. As an extrovert being, Man makes evident sloth and idleness [or *tamas*] through the parasympathetic nerve channel or *ida*, and resourcefulness for sophisticated attachment *[or rajas]* through the sympathetic nerve channel or *pingala*.

In the spinal cord, the first three *chakras [muladhara* or *coccygeal, svadhisthana* or sacral and *manipura* or lumbar] exert their *tamasic* force in Man's affection for wealth, lust and food. The next two *chakras [anhaata* or thoracic and *vishudhha* or cervical] thrust Man towards *rajasic* traits of possessiveness and pride, both of which breed fear of loss. Yet, behind these changeable qualities exists the changeless, imperishable soul that supports the displayed body. He stays in the *kutastha* above the pituitary. Until able to distinguish the *kutastha,* Man is only able to experience the life force and power of God as *prana.*

Man's breath both physical and *prana* emerge from the imperishable *kutastha,* which the seeker reaches by concentrating above the pituitary-hypothalamus. This breath is a substitute under the life force. *Prana* enlivens all *chakras,* the sense organs – in fact the whole body - to pulsate and throb with life and activity.

At every moment, the indwelling individualistic self gives Man varied thoughts and dispositions, according to his tendencies. When Man rises above the perishable body and enters into the sanctuary of the imperishable *kutastha,* he crosses the threshold of immortality to enter the domain of the Soul. After that, every thought brings about a gradual metamorphosis away from old tendencies. A molecular change takes place in the atoms that make up his body's cells. Restoring them with divine energy, he advances towards evolution. Man's coming into this state of being is his preeminent achievement.

When persevering meditation clears the scaffolds across the *ida-pingala,* the *sushumna* channel is clear. *Prana* directly makes a trajectory to the centre of Awareness in the thalamus by passing through the medullary *ajna chakra.* Bathed by agents of transformation from the pituitary and hypothalamus, every cell of the body metamorphoses to a new spirituality. These changes are permanently recorded in the thalamus where *Prakriti* resides in the *kutastha.*

When Man becomes aware he can, all through inspiration, tap into the continuous Bliss of this divine movement, he learns to offer his breath to the Soul. His mind rejoices with the effort. To Man, this is a sign he is making spiritual progress, and with a *guru's* guidance, he can learn to make similar offerings to the seven spiritual *chakras.*

This, however, depends on Man's natural living habits. This, in turn, depends on the correct selection of food, home and company. No other creature eats like Man. Every living thing has its own preferred food. Man alone eats everything. Aided by a superior power of digestion, he taps from the Infinite Reservoir for the sake of indulgence.

But this is a misuse of the power for enjoyment of his senses. It leads to physical and mental illness. *Yogis* insist that Man must be skilful and understand his wants and appetites. Only when he cultivates a taste for peace and contentment can he abandon indulgences. Only then can Man enjoy real happiness. Their advice to seekers:

- Speak less and listen more. Analyse and assimilate what is spoken.
- Practice recharging the divine cave of the brain

and spinal cord. Keep genuine fasts to rest internal organs of the body at least once a week;

- Listen to the Cosmic Vibration that enters through the medulla and always focus your attention at the Cosmic Vision in the *kutastha;*
- Learn and practice deep breathing.

Selfless Action

Only he who abandons the *doing* of all action can be liberated from the Law of *Karma* or action. And to achieve such a state, Man has to be aware of the existence of the seven worlds of names and forms [or *lokas*], associated with the seven *chakras* or stepladder to meditation:

- **Bhuloka** exists in the coccygeal or *muladhara chakra,* from where materialism is offered to the self in the form of wealth and luxuries.
- **Bhuvaloka** exists in the sacral or *svadhisthana chakra,* from where sexual pleasure and offspring are offered to the individualistic self.
- **Svahaloka** exists in the lumbar or *manipura chakra,* wherefrom Man offers food to the fire of digestion, so that the self may partake of it as *prana* or life force to keep the biological body alive.
- **Mahaloka** exists in the thoracic or *anhaata chakra,* where affection is offered to the self through interaction with family, friends, possessions and creatures.
- **Janaloka** exists in the cervical or *vishuddha chakra,* where pride often mars the offering of high idealism to the individualistic self.
- **Tapaloka** exists in the pituitary-medullary brain or *ajna chakra,* where restlessness of envy veils its existence. The seeker offers his incoming breath to this centre, to enliven the biological body.
- **Satyaloka** is located on the top of the brain, ten fingerbreadths from the *kutastha* above the eyebrows. This is the *sahasrahara chakra.* An evolved

> *yogi* enters this domain in a breathless and pulseless state, where the sound of many waters can be heard.

Under the guidance of an evolved preceptor, Man can gain the ability to transform himself from restlessness to self perfection, step by step, from *loka* to *loka*. He gains self-control through breath control. The Soul gradually detaches from the three bodies [physical-astral-causal] and enters the formless stage of Awareness to Consciousness. This is because meditation awakens the divine authority and raises it from the lower centres to the upper centres. When the *yogi* arrives at the centre of Will behind the glabella, he experiences love and joy. Work, after that, is an offering of love, without the attachment for name, fame or ego.

Clearing the Three Nerve Channels

Man often laments spiritual practices are unsuccessful. The prearranged delusory power of Maya and Her triple thrusts through *gunas* make spiritualism difficult for many. Yet, only by detachment through meditation can Man separate himself from the triple qualities of delusion. He must liberate himself from the influence of the three nerve channels - *ida, pingala* and *sushumna.*

The first step is to surmount the *tamasic* tendencies of apathy and inertia. The second is to withdraw from the *rajasic* creativity of the senses, purely for the sake of indulgence. The third step is to involve oneself with a *sattvic* life of spirituality. These steps ensure that there's movement away from the *ida* and *pingala,* becoming centred towards the *sushumna.* Through breath control, gradual control over personal life also emerges. Though most of us obey the impulses of Nature, it is possible to go beyond Nature's compulsions. Seekers, who lead strict, disciplined lives practicing *Kriya Yoga,* can be freed of body consciousness and the influence of the five gross elements [earth, water, fire, air and space]. Through meditative practices as taught by a Master, one can withdraw mindfulness from the lower three centres and into the thoracic and cervical centres.

One who achieves this becomes temporarily free of attentiveness of body, mind and intellect, and discerningly senses the stillness of the unenlightened *chitta* in the fifth centre. Here, Man experiences the peace and joy of an indefinable formless presence. But since the experience has not been permanently fixed, one descends towards the lower centres. He is once more influenced by the power of *Maya.* Intense meditative practice must continue until one goes beyond the pituitary and into the *kutastha*, the reflection of the sixth centre, the *ajna chakra*. By reaching and transcending the sixth centre, Man remains in the *kutastha*. Here one can surpass the triple qualities of *Maya*, provided one rises above the pituitary.

By this time, one understands and experiences the scriptures. He learns about offering one's breath to the Soul. He immerses himself into selfless action. One knows, he has experienced, that *breath proficiency is self-mastery*. One is now able to enter the *sushumna* above the *kutastha*. Here he is neither attached, nor detached. The sense organs do not present a distraction.

Watching inspiration can be tied to a *mantra*. In this manner the mind is immersed in repeating a holy word, such as *AUM [Amen or Amin or Hum]*. When the mind and breath lose their identity, there is arresting of physical breath and life force breath comes from all channels to flow up through the central spinal cord channel or *sushumna*.

This breath is occasional, fine and with no expiratory part. By bringing the *prana* into the *sushumna*, life force is able to enter the *kutastha* above the hypothalamus-pituitary-pineal axis. Man now enters the divine kingdom within the cave of the cranium. While in the *kutastha* he experiences the symphonic adaptation of Heavenly Lights and Sound that emanate from the *chakras*.

From that moment on, a wave becomes the ocean. With the help of a true teacher, Man ascends even higher, leaving behind the temptations of the lower *chakras* until one is in the kingdom of emancipation, and in *samadhi*.

Sage *Vyasa*, the author of the *Bhagavad Gita*, has described how he reached the Ocean of Bliss. First, he had to dissolve his mental faculty into the plexuses or *chakras*. With the practice of drawing up the negative polarity of the first three centres to the positive polarity of the fourth and fifth centres, he creates a median controlled life force. These unite with the stillness and silence. And, while resting in the peacefulness and serenity of the ocean, he advises the chanting of the *gayatri mantra*. Immersion in this *mantra* gives the seeker the grace and wisdom to picture the spiritual eye in the *kutastha*.

Gayatri Mantra

Aum Bhoor Bhuwah Swaha
Tat Savitur Varenyam
Bhargo Devasaya Dhee Mahi
Dhiyo Yo Naha Pracho Dayat

Thou art the Giver of Life
The Remover of pain and sorrow,
The Bestower of happiness –
Creator of the Universe,
May we receive Your supreme –
Sin-destroying Light,
May You guide our intellect in the right direction.

Thousands of Hindus visit the River *Ganga* [Ganges] in Allahabad. [Uttar Pradesh, India] every day. The devout are convinced that a dip in the *Triveni,* the confluence of the three rivers - *Ganga, Yamuna* and *Sarasvati,* the invisible or underground river - will give them emancipation for the next life. This is where the three rivers meet.

Metaphorically, as per *raja-kriya yoga,* the *ida nadi* or parasympathetic channel flows through the left nostril, and She is the *Ganga.* The *pingala nadi* or sympathetic channel flows through the right nostril, and She is the *Yamuna.* The central or spinal cord channel is the *sushumna,* and She is the *Sarasvati.* The confluence of these three nerve channels in the midbrain eventually leads to the ocean of Awareness in the thalamus. From here they merge with pure

Consciousness in the pineal gland in the depths of the *sahasrahara*.

Through *pranayama* or breath control, the practitioner gradually enters this main highway to emancipation, through the *sushumna*. The wanderings of *prana* with uncontrolled breathing must be reeled in by education in *pranayama*. One cannot gain fortitude till breathing and life force are united in the *sushumna*. Further, to ensure this happens smoothly, the practice of harmonizing moral commandments of restraint, to faithfulness heading for Truth and detachment from depravity is necessary.

Man is under the control of Nature and Her powers. Matter includes the elements and the *chitta* [earth, water, fire, air, space, mind, intellect and ego]. Nature's laws instinctively guide Man towards body consciousness. The only way to withdraw from extroversion is to withdraw from the senses, and raise awareness towards the thalamus in the *kutastha*. Here lies the home of Nature's Awareness in the *kutastha*. Once experienced in Her splendour as divinity, peace and bliss, automatic success results in the battle against the power of illusion or Maya. Man then realises he was created to strive for this self-unfoldment and Self-realisation.

Devotion

The body exists because of breath. This breath is God and the power of God. Yet, God is beyond breath. How, then, can Man find God? Essentially, for progressive self-unfoldment to result in Self-realisation, the most important attitude is devotion to the teacher, his teachings and a connection to the Spirit. Only then can Man endorse the tenacity to practice the meditative techniques of *Kriya Yoga.* With every breath, Man must remember to see the power of God ***[Sa - So]*** empowering the body ***[ham].*** Until the act of witnessing the breath becomes a residue in his mental landscape as a constant, ingrained inner awareness, the exploration remains elusive.

Meditation is a spiritual journey from the South to the North. That is, human existence has to be lifted from the southern *muladhara chakra* in the coccyx, to the northern divine location above the pituitary and in the fontanel in the *sahasrahara chakra.* From the domain of money, materialism, lust, desire, food, possessions and pride, the practicing *kriya yogi* reaches real happiness with the experience of being One with the Self. All this happens in the presence of the Soul sun in the thalamus above the pituitary.

Sense organs lie to the front of the spine, in the facade of the human body. And farther external to the body lie temptations of materialism. When engrossed in extrovertedness, the individualistic self is lured through the senses. These beguiling mirages act through smell, taste, sight, sound and touch. When emotionally involved with temptation, the life force heads southwards. Awareness is wrenched towards the coccyx. Man, however, is unaware that he can't attach himself to these incitements unless sanctioned by Nature.

Kriya Yoga teaches Man to move northwards along the spine where no sense organs and, thus, no delusion exist. With inhalation, Man is taught to raise *prana* upbeat along the back of the spine. With exhalation man carries the breath downwards in front of the spine and body. During deeper meditative practice, breath *[swaas]* becomes more *pranic* and infrequent *pranayama* frees the body from *swasayama.* It allows the practitioner to withdraw from the mind and the senses. Through the practice of *jyoti mudra,* Man ascends along the spine to reach the *kutastha.* Here he lingers to witness the divine illumination of the universal being. Here Man finally experiences the unity of **So** and **Sa** with **ham.**

This is the trajectory of self-unfoldment. The *ida* [parasympathetic] and *pingala* [sympathetic] are separated but repeatedly need to retrace the route and the path of the *sushumna.* Once knowledgeable, the seeker enters through a unified tract which opens together into the *kutastha.* This is taught by an experienced teacher as a scientific meditation technique. Spiritual progress is made through intense commitment. Until the life force in the *sushumna* rises northwards, to meet with the *kutastha* above the pituitary, there cannot be Awareness.

Practicing *Kriya Yoga* is obviously more indispensable than just the *bookish knowledge* of this text. This is because knowledge alone is less enduring than transformation through devotion. It now becomes a personal experience. Constant association with one's breath brings about devotion for emancipation of the self. The Soul, which resides at the core of Man's being, prompts self-unfoldment. This now becomes Man's duty.

Man must distinguish those temptations though the extrovert senses are also empowered by the same life force or *prana.* He must entrust life to practicing this path of perfection, of *Kriya Yoga.* This is possible only through devotion and intense sincerity. Once self-unfolded, Man sees the divine illumination in the *kutastha* and hears the divine sound of AUM.

Section V

Spiritual Efforts

Sadhana

Man should strive for fitness and competence. He must do this in material sciences of the world as well as in the science of the Soul. To define this in a worldly context, material science encompasses the workings of a food-dependent mind, intellect and senses. The science of self-unfoldment that leads to Self-realisation is, however, an inward journey that involves self-definition and self-perfection.

The seeker must arrive at inner fitness. A clear vision and freedom from faultfinding conserves energy. This must be done before he embarks on a spiritual journey. When the mind is clear and the seeker begins to notice divinity in everything, he is attracted, spontaneously, to a *guru*. From a *guru* he receives the gift of wisdom. He learns the soul [**sa** and **so**] lives in the brain. **Sa** constantly breathes life up towards Awareness and **so** consciously witnesses **ham** or the body enlivened by **prana.** Man gets taught spiritual practices or *sadhana* about Soul Culture.

But why is the path to spirituality shrouded in mystery? Why is it full of secrets? Many ask the same questions. It is true the Soul is hidden in a secret place. But it must be understood that unless the mind and the intellect are pure, it is impossible to penetrate the furtive *kutastha*. Meditation purifies the mind. When it reaches *no thoughts*, it allows Man to reach *no-mind.* He is now aware of the individualistic self.

The subsequent step is a persistent northward journey in meditation until Man reaches self-unfoldment. Even this, however, is an indirect estimation of the changing individualistic identity. In the midst of a silent mind, Man must shut the doors of his senses and feel the connection between the in-breath pulled into the body by the soul empowered body enlivened by *pranic-breath.*

Self-realisation is a gradual experience. This understanding of the wave can't exist without that of the sea. Man experiencing a wave is nothing else but an understanding of the ocean. The northward journey takes him above the pituitary into the illumination of the *kutastha*. He then travels into the seventh *sahasrahara chakra* in the fontanel. He, the formless Soul understands he is beyond the limitations of the five elements represented in the spinal *chakras*. But again, without the five elements displaying in the *chakras,* and without Matter's inherent qualities, there cannot be Creation or Dissolution. Without wants and dreams, there is no creation. Without deep sleep, there is no dissolution. Man must experience that creation and dissolution are possible because of breath.

Man is engrossed in materialism, wants and rituals that calm the deities of his own *karmic* circumstance. If he instead concentrates on breath being drawn towards the *kutastha* for a long time, he spontaneously develops an indifference and detachment from objects, emotions and thoughts. With his attention above the pituitary, he can change to a hermit like existence. Here he is preoccupied with inner tranquillity. With thorough control over emotions, thoughts, intellect and ego, he witnesses unity in all multiplicity. In this calm state, he conserves his energy and inner strength for a better health. *Kriya Yoga* is best practiced after all, with a sound physical-physiological-psychological body.

Laws of Prosperity and Success

Success in life is a result of obeying Nature's laws. It becomes stylised in material achievement and meeting life's needs. The ambition to make money should, therefore, be coupled with a want for comfort for others. And this subliminal obligation should underscore all of Man's successes. Those who ignore, or disbelieve, this rule fail to use divine resources intelligently. Undermining Man's immortal heritage is against the Laws of Nature and Her bounty.

Every religion issues strict warning against acts that violate other beings' personal space and awareness, or even their sins. Some seekers, even while on the path to spirituality, continue such violations. But if every seeker adheres to *yama* and *niyama,* Man obeys virtue. He must stay away from *kama* [or passion and lust], *krodha* [or anger], *lobha* [or greed], *moha* [or infatuation], *mada* [or pride], *matsarya* [or envy], *aalasya* [or sloth] and *ahamkar* [or ego]. These tendencies are also distinctly defined in other faiths. They are called the *Seven Deadly Sins.* Moses repeated identical Ten Commandments for Eastern and later Western civilizations.

- **Lust** or passion is wanting without regard for the needs of another. It stems from lack of respect for others and, eventually, for oneself.
- **Greed** is the urge to take, without giving back to either Man or Nature. It breeds the death of generosity, and could lead to the end of cooperation in the world.
- **Gluttony** is over-consumption of Nature's gifts [be it food or Nature's resources] that can't be exhausted, but should be left for future generations.

- **Pride** and arrogance is the feeling that one, alone, deserves the gifts of the Earth.
- **Jealousy** is the wish to own what others have, a negativity that kills self-growth and motivation in life.
- The working man considers idleness and **Sloth** a virtue. He refuses to work, but demands more for himself. He destroys his personal responsibility and will to survive without this power.
- **Greed** is the deadly combination of spite, hate, greed, gluttony, lust and jealousy. With it, Man projects his need to destroy all with the shadow of his own failings.

These tendencies are earned through many previous lives. It is important to transcend them for the sake of balance in one's own life. In a macrocosmic sense, a balanced culture in world society must be the code of ethics. The balance between giving and receiving, planting and harvesting, taking from the Earth and giving back to Her is a sign of balanced societal culture. Balance between oneself and others, between inner values and outer expression is balanced soul culture. For Man, it is as much about feast and fast, silence and speech, freedom and self-restraint, creative action and inspirational thought. And, of course, time to seek God and time to let God be clear within is necessary also.

In the Circle of Life, fulfilment of the body, mind, intellect and *vasanic* or causal wants gives Man his creative urge to live and strive. But the rules are clear. The interaction of Man's want must be for and within Nature's laws. When Man violates any of the seven Matter sheaths [physical-astral-causal], it results in death and disease in that sheath during his lifetime. In addition, these violations are carried forward as *karmic* loads into future lives.

Evolution

They say prosperity in its many forms is necessary as a tool in evolution. If Man does not have the means to satisfy his wants, these cravings become a preference over virtue. He then over-seeks, finally losing himself to materialism. There is, of course, nothing wrong with wealth and prosperity. But there is something erroneous when one becomes fanatical with it. Obsessions express in a selfish primitive mind. On the other hand, those who earn more should give more. By reducing disparity and imbalance, Man restores a collective point of view. Charity is a privilege. It is a rare gift few come by. It presents as an opportunity to physically serve mankind. Man must develop the mental strength to devote time to others. He must share his tangible possessions.

The quality of self-satisfaction depends on the stability of a silent mind and controlled respiration. Meditation can help Man achieve calmness, satisfaction, inner contentment and harmony. This allows a balanced personal growth. It is consistent with spiritual ascent. Such a lifestyle enables Man to plan for the present and the future. His changing is of clear thinking and logic. There is lucidity. An organised lifestyle governs the realms of materialism.

On the other hand, the lower centres – especially an over stimulated third chakra – throw Man into a ferocious pressure group inculcating terror. Inner poise and self-control are replaced with chronic anxiety. Worry, galloping imagination and the belief that *problems are everywhere* are his hallmarks. He becomes prone to committing blunders. Frustrated, he finds himself not meeting with his own expectations.

Patience, not only with others but also with himself, is

the balm. His temperament and qualities are gifts of his nature. They evolve through many previous births. Even in daily activities, Nature will take its own direction. And though Man may make a conscious effort to change, manipulate and achieve his ambitions, he does not meet with success. His actions cannot consummate in a specific reward. For dividends come with different faces. They depend on Man's will and grace of the Soul.

Calm lower centres have the ability and power to stabilise other centres. Peace is the essential ingredient for Man to prosper at any, and every, level. This combines, and intertwines with the blessings of the Mother of Eight Wealth. They include prosperity, trust as non-suspiciousness, dignity, spiritual ascent, pure knowledge, and domestic and collective joy, wealth and success.

On a physical level, attitudes towards food and eating habits are an aptitude taught by wise mothers. Any dysfunctional attitudes in this arena result in problems of the stomach. Diseases develop from the dyspeptic breakdown and absorption of undigested food molecules into the liver. Over time this affects Man's gross body. Therefore, indiscriminate fasting, as well as overindulgence and increased frequency in food intake, disturbs the neurological works of the lower *chakras.*

Fasting has been used for millenniums to control Man's thoughts, for thoughtless meditation. For many, however, fasting is a habitual rite, without any purpose. That is of no help, and if one continues to fast for more than forty days, it can lead to digesting the body's organs. One must remember the world's objects are for controlled enjoyment, not indulgence. One can enjoy Nature's gifts, but must control one's thoughts through breath control.

Remaining Connected

As Man aspires for materialistic and spiritual success, the vagaries of his mind, his physical body and the circumstances that surround him impose limits on him. Often, his efforts are half-hearted. Or he may turn to despair, which arrests his willpower. But a seeker of divine quality must remain connected to the *mains* of divine Will. He must make out the power of God in his own speech and ensure every word is truthful yet sensitive.

Disciplined in life and fully self-controlled, the seeker creates the infrastructure for materialistic and spiritual activity. Being fully connected he surrenders all activity to **sa,** the indwelling soul. He experiences **ham** as his own physical expression and that of Creation's. He understands that his body and soul are One. He feels this unity with the world, with every plant, creature and thing.

No longer does the seeker remain in the southern *chakras*. He rises to the pituitary and beyond. He is connected to His presence in every breath and with every thought. Sincere devotion to the journey and *guru* allows him to ignite his ego in the fire of personal experience. When breath has matured to become fine and subtle, the seeker watches the divine illumination in the *kutastha* and hears the cosmic sound.

When he opens his eyes to multiplicity, he sees it, and him, living in the womb of Nature. He understands, intuitively, the Spirit *[Purusha]* empowers Matter *[Prakriti]*. This happens whether slothful, creative or in blissful harmony. He knows this with every breath. He feels the Spirit, the compassionate silent witness. He sees the physical breath changed to *prana* for Creation. Whether Man is awake or dreaming *Purusha* and *Prakriti* become the eternal seed in Dissolution. Man is now in deep sleep.

Watching the breath, constantly, is true meditation. After that, the Spirit regulates and controls the entire meditating seeker. Deep in meditation and in *kechri mudra* [the tongue rolled into the roof of the mouth], the *kriya yogi* tastes *soma* or life's nectar dripping on to the tip of his tongue from the *sahasrahara.* This makes him calm and fulfilled with life's plenty. His spiritual tendencies are magnified. He is eventually able to see himself as the imperishable soul. With his effort, the individualised self has undergone unfoldment and, finally, experienced this Self-realisation.

Now, the seeker has understood that human activity depends on where, and through what, desire is channelled. That is, on the strength of *prana* and its direction through one of three channels or *nadis* coursing the spinal cord. When *prana* flows mostly in the parasympathetic channels or *ida,* the slothful Man has no wish for divinity. When the flow is mostly through the sympathetic channel or *pingala,* it triggers restlessness, activity for indulgence and physical disease. When a *kriya yogi* succeeds in separating the *ida* and *pingala,* by destroying all crossbars, he has reached some success. The central channel or *sushumna* is nearly clear. And *prana* courses through a path of harmony and self-control. This is so necessary for spiritual living.

Desire, the Seed of Restlessness

Desire, be it for materialism or spirituality, is the seed of restlessness. It manifests in Man's emotions, thoughts and his activities. Emotions are the biggest *stumbling blocks* in the seeker's life, clouding him with pride, false modesty, vanity, drive and competitiveness. Though spiritual activity allows him to enjoy peace, it is not permanent. He gravitates to his old ways. Only those who concentrate their thoughts and breath into the three channels can continue the northern journey towards spirituality.

Yes, people get what they strive for. But spiritual life is not a temporary condition. Sudden burning ambition, even for spirituality, leaves the seeker restless. A spiritual life must be continuous. It is with each breath, in every moment. To be freed of restless thought, meditation must be engaged through the channels. Deep sleep is a silhouette of meditation, without awareness. *Kriya Yoga* is meditation with complete awareness. Here, Man's awareness, eventually, dissolves in divine awareness. This happens just as salt is integral to the sea.

The steps of meditation, and the consequent evolution, include freedom from restless thought through breath control. Perceiving divinity within is seeing the illumination at the *kutastha.* Outside, there is a constant experience of being One with Creation. The seeker must learn to recognise the One, the Soul. Man should recognise the flow of breath in every plant, thing and creature. *Prana* is because of which the senses, the sense organs and the *chakras* function. It is this *prana* that invent want and directs it to fruition. Those who cannot decipher this merely exist. They are compelled by past actions *[karma]* and tendencies *[vasanas].*

Foundations of Spiritual Unfoldment

Disciplines of the body, mind and speech are the foundations of spiritual unfoldment. Perseverance in this sphere allows the yogi to be *sattvic.* His whole being goes into harmony with his true Self. With intense meditation, he works at his behaviour from WITHIN. He earns virtues of the body, mind and speech. He worships Nature's expressions. And he pays homage to the Spirit. The creative power of Nature communicates with Man in meditation. Most importantly, his actions are pure, honest, sincere and desireless, and intend no harm.

The seeker's speech is disciplined, supported by an inner opinion of the truth. This penetrates his conscious, subconscious and unconscious states. In meditation while deep in his causal being, he enters his previously unconscious being with super-consciousness He experiences the Truth. With continued deep meditation, he increasingly becomes One with this Truth. His speech is kind, forceful and truthful *[satyam],* wise and pleasant *[priya]* and valuable *[hitam].* His speech breeds peace, understanding and well being and is free of harsh connotations. Ecstatic meditation gives the mind tranquil, placid and content.

The ego transformed is trained to encourage quietness. This gradual inner purification makes the seeker want the same in all outer action as well. Thus, all his actions embody a divine purity.

The seeker understands the Law of Karma. He knows that attachment to his attainments binds the Soul in their expression. He frees himself from the longings of the fruits of his actions through renunciation first. He meditates deeply to become One with God. Even if he fails, the seeker never stops seeking Him.

With every wave of each thought, with faith and perseverance, he sinks down into the depths of the deep-sea. He knows he is in himself, until he destroys the barrier of past lives. Eventually, he becomes One with the Cosmic Ocean. He now not only renounces all fruits of action but he relinquishes them as acts of God alone. The result of this reverberates into the Universe designed for a Collective and Cosmic Good.

Ambitions

Materialistic ambitions are preordained qualities or *gunas.* They are passions of destinies *[vasanàs]* hidden in Man and are great obstacles. The seeker must defeat them and stifle the pull of extroverted existence. Through meditation, he learns how to *introvert* the senses. An automatic shedding of tendencies frees him of anxiety, pitfalls and worry. These come about as Man reaches pure Awareness in the thalamus, above the pituitary. He feels Nature's generous presence, and the necessities of past inclinations. He also wants to be with Her.

To transcend worldly existence, the seeker invokes his breath towards *prana* and draws the breath through the nose and into the thalamus. He gradually forgets his worldly existence. By timing his inspiration with ***sa,*** Man watches the witnessing power of the Spirit as ***so*** permeate the biological body ***ham.***

The mystical thoracic or *anahaata chakra* is symbolic of the real underlying soul-intuition of Man. It has the capacity to give or receive unconditional love from the Cosmic Mother. But Man does not and cannot sense it. Possessiveness and attachment to things and beings cancels the blessing of the Breath.

Through correct interaction with Creation, Man can gain the power to heal himself. A *voice* from within tells Man he has the knowledge of all his past lives. But once he desires to be One with Him, he aligns all these wants and becomes a channel of *prana* or life force. He, then, patterns his outer world in exact accordance with images that are filled in his slowly transforming causal being. He uses his body, mind, intellect and the unenlightened soul *[chitta]* to live his life correctly. His life, then, becomes a journey of responsibility.

The central nervous system is the final common pathway through which all knowledge of life is received. The *rishi* [Spirit] or experiencer **watches** integrating new input into the *devata* [Matter]. As Man wills for a wished experience, Nature **looks** on and supervises all changes being made within Her body [thalamus]. The master organs [hypothalamus and pituitary] are commanded to oversee the release of transformed neurohormones and neurotransmitters. The target body cells change old cells. All following afferent input is a transformed experience. The efferent experience has a specific *[chhandas]* quality to equal the value of the afferent stimulus.

Man's central nervous system is designed to change through the power of his will. Therefore, Will, as the Creator is the omnipotent Being. In seeking the Creator in the *kutastha,* Man becomes omniscient and omnipresent. Once Man wishes immortality, his thoughts must be transformed through meditation. He must discover Infinity through regular and intense practice of *Raja-Kriya yoga.* The seeker must continue a self-evaluation over years. He discovers that he, the mortal, and the Cosmic Mother are One. He is the Son - *Purusha* of the Father- *Purushotama* and She - *Prakriti,* the Holy Spirit.

He must divert his outgoing currents inwards and northwards into the divine cave. There he will find Her. A synthesis of his emotions and his thoughts, as they align with this flow of life force, leads to transformation of his body structures. This happens starting within the DNA molecule. The distance between outgoing life force *[apana]* and incoming life force *[prana]* gradually shortens. There is gradual but complete synthesis within the astral being, especially in the *sushumna.*

Man continues to misinterpret scriptures. The sages or prophets of religion advise Man to first reduce the gap between physical *[tamasic]* demands and creative *[rajasic]* actions. Once harmony of *sattva* becomes fixed, Man can transcend all these qualities. He fixes himself in the temple of God in the *kutastha.*

Housing God in churches, temples and mosques is valued more than finding Him within. Distance and division is created between Man and God by humanity. Isn't separation from God the cause for family and societal disruption? The blind Mind must uplift itself to Man's identification with Him. In His altar within the divine cave, witnessing God as a Collective Supreme Consciousness becomes every person's divine right. All must meditate together at this altar within. The result surely will be the Intuitive Vision of togetherness, in harmony. This harmony allows for Universal Oneness and non-destruction.

Ego in the Zone of War

In the epic *Mahabharata,* the battlefield was *Kurukshetra.* The combat was between cousins. One hundred evil *Kauravas* fought five virtuous *Pandavas* for integrity. *Kaurava* princes encouraged by their blind father King *Dhritarashtra* followed a life of extrovert wants, satisfaction, gluttony, possessiveness, pride, jealousy and individuality. The grandfather *Bheeshma,* although righteous, reeked of unpleasant individuality. He could choose his time of death. This Ancient Royal Parent *Bheeshma,* an incarnate Ego, was gifted with a celestial boon. He would live as long as he wanted.

Krishna, a divine Son of God, became *Arjuna's* charioteer. *Arjuna* spent many years practicing the art of warfare *[yoga]* against extrovert senses. *Yama* and *niyama* followed by *abhyas* made *Arjuna* an expert on breath and thought control.

Challenging each other on the battlefield of *Kurukshetra,* the chosen war zone was the five southern *chakras* in the spinal cord. The evil cousins overcrowded to subdue the five cousins with the power of one hundred horses pulling in every direction.

Armed with virtues of meditation, *Arjuna* with the help of his army was able to fell *Bheeshma.* There had to be harmony among the *Pandavas.* Their efforts needed unification with divine will. Guidance was given by the Universal Intelligence of *Krishna.* Until combat conditions were perfected, the egoistic *Bheeshma* could not be defeated. The bloodiest of wars followed. The battle continued until *Bheeshma* agreed to be killed. Ego needed a joint decision, to die. The mind, intellect, and individuality as *chitta* personality surrendered in unison to such destruction.

Ego continues to be the greatest obstacle to spiritual evolution. It is an obstacle to Man's liberation and is also the cause of his bondage. Attached to activities and fruits of action he is unable to renounce action nor able to relinquish their reactions. Whenever Man acts, ego becomes the agency as doer. Ego denies action in Man is mediated through the power of breath or *prana* - the only power of a doer.

However, once outgoing senses are transcended through *pranayama,* thought control is achieved in meditation. The battlefield is cleared of inert *tamasic ida*-centred tendencies and *rajasic pingala*-focused restlessness of creativity. All intrusions by sympathetic-parasympathetic channels are cleared. Harmonious *sattvic* forces give Man freedom. The pathway to rise in the *sushumna* through the higher *chakras* is clear. Man transcends senses and tendencies. The northward journey is into the altar of the *kutastha,* above the pituitary.

To sum up, there is no suppression of sensory demand, only transformation in thought. The angelic forces in the fourth and fifth plexuses are brought closer to the lower three negative centres until harmony prevails between them. The opposing forces at the spinal cord's two poles - the negative pole at the coccygeal plexus above the anus and the positive pole in the bosom at the fifth plexus - are brought together. Physical breath control is transformed by *pranayama. Prana* enlivens the physical expression even in breathlessness.

Dexterous skill is needed to shift the flow of the *ida* and *pingala* nervous systems, and to clear the median force of the *sushumna.* The shift occurs at the mystical third plexus, as *prana* rises to the fourth plexus. It remains stagnant here, unless lifted to the fifth plexus in the throat. The next upward movement is from the throat to the medullary plexus, where the causal being reigns and resides. This ascending journey is towards *Dharmakshetra,* the battlefield of goodness. This is also the home of super-consciousness above the pituitary, in the domains of Awareness and Consciousness. For all this to happen, a *guru* is needed.

The physical location of *Dharmakshetra,* on the top of the brain, is pointed to in the ancient *Purusha Suktam* with the following verse:

Aum sahas sra shiir shaa purusha
saha sraakshah saha sra paat
sa bhumin vishvato vrit va
atyata tishta dash aangulam

Oh Infinite Lord, who is awarded with a thousand heads, eyes and feet and fills the Universe, who is in Every Atom of Expression from Here to Eternity, You can be found in me [my brain] between the *kutastha* to ten finger-breaths above it [the crown of the head]

Reaching Deathlessness in Meditation

Man must learn to conquer sloth and sleep. Once he does, he can meditate deeply and for long periods of time. By using the ***HAM SA SO HAM*** mantra, he can concentrate on His power being drawn automatically by the sixth centre in the medulla or *ajna chakra.* The *entrance to God* is reflected in the *kutastha* by the occipital lobe. If Man concentrates on the *kutastha* behind the two eyebrows with each inspiratory ***sa,*** he knows, intuitively, that he is being enlivened by ***so*** with each breath. Gradually, he can command his soul-identified being to focus on his spiritual being. It is within the divine cave in the thalamus. This spiritual view of the *third eye* sets up the prized stage of meditation.

Man can now be sure to free himself from the grip of the Law of Qualities *[gunas].* Its effect on intuition is a loosening grip of *Maya's* delusory power. Next, he gradually separates himself from his sense-inflamed outgoing mind that drags him towards objects, emotions, and things [OET]. The pull of three *tamasic* centres that claim money and materialism, sexual indulgence and food is placed wilfully on the back burner. At a leisurely pace detachment starts. With it fear, attachment, anger, sorrow, greed, pride, arrogance and doubt loosen their grip. As he hankers for balance and peace, Man becomes more established in meditation.

His personal experience of intuitive knowledge allows him to transcend the *rajasic* fourth and fifth *chakras.* They gradually release their hold on him. He understands his actions are expressions of Nature. At this point, he is beyond the swinging *gunas* of inertia and creativity. Man seeks harmony. The life force gradually rises through the subtle spiritual centres *[chakras]* towards the *ajna* or medullary centre. This upward direction of flow triggers not just intense desire to be One with the Spirit, but also distaste for materialism.

Even sporadic tries at deep meditation can lead Man to a rich sense of peace and joy in the sixth *sattvic ajna* centre in the medulla. The frequency, length and depth of his meditative effort decide the greatness and duration of this spiritual perception. Man knows he must move up further, above the pituitary. He must endure in the *kutastha* within the thalamus. This underlies the second stage of meditation.

Man, now keenly aware of the importance of *yama* [restraints] and *niyama* [adherence to restraints], arrives at the midpoint of his spiritual journey *[sadhana]*. Having glimpsed *ananda* or Bliss, in tiny experiences, Man realises Awareness exists within him. It is not in worldliness but in his assembled being in the divine cave. With faith, he meditates even harder, since he now knows how it gets done.

In the last stage of meditation, Man takes his spiritual opinion into the halls of perfect Awareness and Consciousness. The sacred place is above the pituitary, between the thalamus and the crown of the head in the fontanel. Here he must wait for the final union of the Self and the Supreme Spirit. Once beyond the influence of his individuality of self, personal and social wants, likes-and-dislikes and habits do not bind him. He is beyond the compulsions of Maya. He has transcended her, which prompts towards delusion. *Gunas* of matter embedded in the first five *chakras* of the divine cave have no jurisdiction over the self now changing into the Self.

Yet, the greatest battle still awaits Man. Because his personality or *chitta* [mind-intellect-ego complex] lives in the sixth centre, ego poses a challenge. His meditative techniques can help him control and transform the mind and intellect, but he must obliterate the ego. Even advanced *yogis* are dragged down if the ego is not defeated. Only by merging *Shakti* [Energy of Awareness] with *Shiva* [Light of

Consciousness] can the ego be overcome. Success is a matter of faith and the teacher's grace.

The knowledgeable seeker, completely aware of this crisis, charts out the next step in his *sadhana.* Knowing he must invoke deep dispassion, he meditates even deeper. He re-examines all that he has studied throughout his life, so he can face the unavoidable combat with ego. Survival instinct of ego is born of Nature. Therefore the mythical duality of Awareness and Consciousness, meaning Matter and Spirit, or *Me* and *I* can only be fought through spiritual determination and self-control.

The help of a true *guru* and his benevolence, therefore, must be sought. Man needs a Master's guidance and encouragement for his self-evolution. The student has an instinctive tendency to become dependent on the Master. Man must dig deep within himself for knowledge. It is already there. It needs uncovering through austerity and meditation.

The seeker should be warned that acts of deep meditation reawaken habits and tendencies that previously lay in slumber or were ignored. Their potency increases with ego fierce resistance. Despite a growing power of awareness and discrimination, the seeker is distressed and confused. Unfavourable tendencies such as gloominess, moodiness or anger re-appear. Replace these tendencies and habits with newer, positive habits of peace, calmness through concentration *[dharana]* that are the restorative cure.

The eternal questions about the relevance of Matter and Spirit must also be re-answered. As he overcomes flaws in his understanding, the seeker asks the same troubling questions. Queries come from different levels of understanding. Each level is an expansion over the previous. When *prana* withdraws from the senses and is transferred to the divine cave, he senses victory over inferior body sensations. Sensory demands will gradually dissolve. He must continue his outward conventional duties work, but remain inwardly united in Bliss. The portrayal of life acquires a new meaning. The intricately organised scenes are dream-plays of God [*lilas*]. Man must concentrate on serving Nature. In the whirlpool of activity, he sees thc vibration-less infinitude of eternal Bliss - the Many from the One.

Restlessness, the cause of all suffering, is the result of irregular breathing patterns. Those who can calm the breath through *Kriya Yoga* are freed of restlessness and unhappiness. Man does not withhold breath of *swasayama* uncomfortably, he only transforms it with *pranayama.*

The advanced yogi, who has complete breath control, doesn't breathe while he meditates. He has reached a breathless, pulseless stage. He has reached a deathless stage. Here he requires nothing. He sees the power of the One in every thought. He looks on the frenzied world with compassion and detachment. He realises that everything is activated by His power and understands, intuitively, there is no duality. Discrimination or differentiation in the Doer does not exist. He only enlivens everything and everyone. In His omnipresence, He is the same in everything and equally present in all. But to reach this inner understanding, there has to be devotion to teacher and consistency in *sadhana.*

Analysing Knowledge

Man has deep regard for intellect, especially for objective knowledge. He interprets everything according to the facts and figures he has in his memory. To the materialist, this is Knowledge. But Man has rarely inferred that his intellect depends on the senses and their contact with the world.

Each aspect of his being is involved in what Man does. His body obeys instructions. It receives messages through images in his mind. His emotions, too, are triggered by these representations. It is such portrayals stoking the fires of his life force. His mind patterns his thoughts. Mind gives shape only to especially chosen reflections. And these images speak to him constantly. As *inner voice* it recounts the shape and form, based on his past action. The changing script, as a result, becomes his present life.

Meditation helps Man change these reproductions. The body, mind and intellect [BMI] undergo adjustment through transformation. What happens is that everything outside himself [OET: objects-emotions-thoughts], as well as his perceptual representations, undergo change. This continues until they become a reflection of his transformed inner being. He realises that he is connected to all things big and small. He now chooses to change, for the good of the whole. By it, he can move towards what is good for his own life as well.

This search for Knowledge is endless. Man wants to know everything. His search ends only when he discovers the Knowledge of the Soul, away from the external world.

The intellect, also gifted with desire and ambition, is not restless and confused like the mind. It has the ability to rise above the mind. It enters the sphere of rationality. It has the ability to lead Man to the Soul, the source of everything. As intellect gives birth to Knowledge, it moves to higher states of awareness. Eventually it arrives at the Self-revealing wisdom through scientific *Kriya Yoga.*

When Man concentrates *[dharana]* and meditates *[dhyana],* he moves beyond the reasoning thoughts. He sees and witnesses thought awareness, until thought dies away. He becomes aware of personal, intuitive knowing that is free from the amassed data of past knowledge.

This involves understanding that intuitive knowing works in a limited way through the mind and intellect. But it is and will remain an independent knowing. His intelligence is the light of his mind and intellect.

The intellect cannot work without the power of intuition in intelligence behind it. Universal Intelligence cannot express unless both Matter and Spirit are united. Neither Christ nor *Krishna,* for that matter, none of the prophets who came as *Sons* of God, could have expressed God's message. The Knowledge they spread would be a *mission impossible.* Unless the Holy Spirit enlivens and mothers all energy in Matter, no Son who took the form of Man could lead civilization.

Watching the Self

When Man first starts true meditation, he faces restlessness and thought disturbances. These originate from the bottom of the heart or *anhaata chakra.* When he lifts awareness to the neck and above, he achieves calmness. But Man achieves self-control only through breath control. According to sages, there are fifty-two types of breathing beyond which lies the *breathless breath of spirituality.* This *pranayama* is moving *prana,* a fine, tranquil, cool life force. When Man carries his being into this breath through *Kriya Yoga,* he can enter the *kutastha.* By enduring here for a long time, he experiences the brilliance of a million suns in the darkness of space.

Physical and mental self-control without Self-realisation only temporarily distances Man from sense attractions. His mind continues to mull on temptations until he re-succumbs. But he has a safety net. The supreme experience within the *ajna chakra* allows him to transcend *Maya* and Her compulsions. Once he has experienced the bliss of such freedom, he wants to unload all loads. Man loses interest in pleasures of the senses, habits and wants. He takes his *chitta* personality to the Centre of Awareness [thalamus] above the pituitary.

Renunciants must become yogis, lest they lose sight of the divine goal of soul-Spirit union. Outward renunciation, without learning to withdraw *prana* from the senses *[pratyahara],* is unlikely to lead to spirituality. Rather, it can cause inner torment. Memory of pleasures of senses lies dormant in Man's subconscious mind. The sensuous tentacles of desire have drained many a wise man. Man must forever guard himself against signs of greed, temptations of the flesh, love for physical beauty and the need for flattery and indulgence. He should have the ability to destroy these tendencies. But never must Man underestimate the power of his subconscious mind.

Even a wise man with unfulfilled wants can succumb to feelings of egoistic anger that cloud his intellect. It forces him to become increasingly irrational. He can develop righteous indignation and lose his inner balance. Since he undergoes gradual physiological and psychological change these changes are lethal to spiritually. He begins to lose memory of what he must do and how he must behave.

As feelings of beneficent sentiments fade, his capacity to discriminate disappears. He loses contact with his own Awareness. He must, therefore, sublimate and not subdue his sense attractions. He must identify want and ensure the discriminating intellect's thoughts steer and transcend every demand of the sensory mind, until smothered.

Man may find it difficult to think beyond his past habits, grievances, mistakes, hardships and trauma. A positive way to deal with this is to grasp that memory is compost useful for growth in his current spiritual journey, growing inside him. Nurturing the garden of present delight will transform the mind and empower him to live in his new memory.

This rich life-experience will guide his present. Thus freed from the past, he looks at life from a new perspective. This reprogramming and rearrangement supports him. It becomes subtle commands from his subconscious. He becomes ruler of his own reality.

Wisdom

The seeker's transformed image has the abilities of leadership and qualities of kindness and generosity. He can assume the roles of peacemaker, diplomat or counsellor. His vision becomes plain for all to see. He does not have to give commands. He has the wisdom to walk with the flow of life force. He begins to regard inclinations and abilities of those around him with compassion. He gains the wisdom to encourage self-expression of inherent qualities and tendencies in others. He makes others feel *fulfilled.* Adding to his new potential is old wisdom, which gives momentum to that which is already happening.

Having gained control of his senses through discrimination, he ascends the lower five chakras. The seeker watches inhaled oxygen offered into the fire of the Self in the *kutastha.* The pure Soul burns this into *prana.* It is ready to energise and enliven the biological body. Man automatically sheds every entanglement, even as he performs his duties. He owns Soul happiness. His discrimination receives a Soul-force of intuition. Intuitive guidance becomes his wisdom. This guides the intellect to correct reasoning.

Those who refuse to live according to dictates of peace born of the *kutastha* get entangled, again, with the senses. They lose direction, moving away from the goal of life. Discriminating intellect is misused. Pride and a personal sense of accomplishment – hallmarks of the ego – develop instead. Only a few understand that Soul-happiness is an expression of Man's own intelligence. It is the Self. It is Universal Intelligence. It is experienced in the *kutastha chaitanya.*

The *yogi* reasons that his conviction is instinctive and

latent in him. He knows he must awaken his total intuition. The *sadhak* [seeker], who knows both sense-inclinations and Soul-happiness, wheels a standard. He knows wisdom has no comparison. It is nonexistent for the worldly man.

The deeply meditating *sadhak* understands that he must, first, practice physical withdrawal. By detaching from his senses he arrives at the altar of the divine cave. Next, he must be able to watch incoming breath while remaining connected to the Cosmic Vision. Then, he must listen to the Cosmic Vibration of AUM within himself.

He now enters the eye of Cosmic Vision and the sound of the Cosmic Sound. He stays here until he stops hearing the voice of the senses.

Finally, he rises above the astral sounds of his astral spine *[chakras]*. It is only then that he hears AUM within and without. He also sees the Cosmic Light that he must penetrate. On entering the Light, he draws into Cosmic Consciousness.

Harnessing Wisdom

To the Modern Man, *money* is power and therefore, it can never be enough. To a wise man, money is a force that allows him make wise choices and increase the potential of creating benefits for a common good.

To the modern man, *time* is meant for indulgence and pleasure. To the wise man, every moment counts... to love, to create, to strengthen his own Will and search for the Self.

The creative force of *thought* is obvious in the outer world. The wise man takes command of his thoughts in meditation and changes the inner patterns of his thinking. He now translates them to the outer world.

The wise man treats every *loss* and failure as new freedom. It is a gift of new life-opportunity, to refine his effort at self-perfection. This perfected skill, in turn, allows Nature to rechannel the energy for greater common good. The wise man teaches those around him, taking command of life force is better than embracing a struggle. He bridges his views of the outer world. With his *guru's* support, he begins to understand Nature's wholeness.

The Universal Teacher and *Guide* understand the protocol of every life-situation and life-change, in darkness or at dawn. The *guru* guides the seeker through every life-dance. He reveals all things sacred. Calling the seeker's inner being he structures the necessary changes. The seeker's heart knows he has made the right changes and choices.

Over time, the *Light* of a Universal Teacher washes away the personality of the *guru* whom the seeker has known physically. It is replaced by an inner intuitive opinion. The seeker discovers everything that emerges from the Light is the *Total Guru*. He is materialised *Shiva-Shakti* [Spirit and Matter]. He is Universal Intelligence easily seen by a meditating seeker in the Krishna or Christ Centre in the *kutastha*.

The seeker's reasoning is fixed on the *Soul*. He gains the light of Soul-happiness. He is in Bliss, whether he is in meditation or while he serves the world. He has educated his intellect with knowledge. But his *intelligence* needs the light of *intuition*. Intuitive guidance is obvious as *wisdom*. It guides his intellect to do the right thing. The seeker now earns peace or stillness of the body and mind. He is free to enjoy the stillness and silence in meditation.

Sometimes, even those who have progressed along the spiritual path may be distracted from awareness. But discrimination of the intellect and self-control through more intense effort helps Man hold an iron grip on thoughts. He who conquers the blind emotional mind abandons all entanglement with materialism. And once the attraction and aversion of senses is abandoned, they can continue to perform all their worldly duties.

Nature and Worship

We live in a world that is unbalanced. We have mindlessly and relentlessly drained and abused earth's natural resources, with no thought of restoration or replenishment. Yet, the Mother knows how to readjust to such cruelty. She can destroy exhausted landmasses and create new ones through dissolution. Ancient wisdom outlines that most destructions occur where Man has harmed Her physical body the most.

Nature's laws are powerful, in which remains Her own divine plan, even though Man may continue to work against it. Her greatest generosity to Man is seeds of re-creation. These need replanting in the spaces of Her body. The Mother will not regenerate what Man has poisoned. Instead, She transforms the poison and dissolves the poisoned areas with the powers of Her phenomenon. These take the form of earthquakes, floods, fires, storms, the wind and hurricanes, not to mention magnetic and gravitational suctioning into Her womb. The Law of Karma is impeccable.

Man continues to harm Nature. He refuses understanding that the universe is a living, breathing and moving Whole, like any other body. Nature heals that which Man injures. She severs that which is irretrievably injured. She responds in kind when Her subjects are collectively injured. She destroys nations, if the need arises.

The ordinary person worships Nature with flowers, fruit, beauty and intellect. An intelligent being that is self-regulated in spiritual life, however, realises God's presence everywhere. While living in this truth, Man is full of devotion. Because he hears His presence in Her constantly. Man thus becomes one with Mother Nature. He has neither pride nor emotion. He lives to serve the Mother. All his activities are acts of worship.

In this state of self-satisfaction, the intelligent being sees and experiences peace, joy and bliss. His movements to the negative gradually disappear. He is freed from doubts, anxieties, worries and delusions. Through soul culture, he fixes his unity with the Cosmic Mother.

As Awareness *[Prakriti* or Energy] and Consciousness [*Purusha* or Light] unite in Matter, creation and materialisation takes place. This is the power of creativity in creation. The Light of Consciousness remains as the eternal witness, incapable of functioning without the help of Her elements or energy.

It is She who comforts. It is by Her Will she dissolves that which is exhausted. It is the Holy Spirit who is the organizer of creation. She agrees to every need and want, be it plant, creature or humankind. Ignorance that She is a living, breathing, feeling, thinking Mother is lost to civilisation.

Healing

The deluded Man, blinded by the individualistic self, thinks of himself as a limited being. He imagines himself a being weak in the face of difficulties and life's problems. Body conscious, he exhibits fear of suffering, disease and death, unaware that he is imperishable and owns a deathless soul.

The causal-astral body holds the knowledge and experience template of all of Man's previous lives and a memory bank of information of his materialistic and spiritual journeys. Every atom of human expression recalls the search for every pleasure for indulgence, that *prana* in the subtle body was harnessed for a wished purpose, even though Man does not recall that he is enlivened by the power of breath, every atom saves this knowledge. Man is only vaguely aware that his body is a temple of the Soul. He imagines God as a structure somewhere outside himself and in the outer world - in the sky.

If a guru tells him that God is formless and that creation is his structure, Man finds the notion difficult to accept as true. Belief is, therefore, the first step to spiritual practice. Building on this infrastructure of belief is the second step. Man, then, learns *Kriya Yoga* and strives to come up as far as the *ajna chakra,* above the pituitary. While in this state of gradual self-unfoldment, he realises he has been living in the lower centres for satisfaction of the senses. He meditates by healing and energising the body, mind and intellect. Transforming his body comes as a surprise to him. He begins to accept the constant change that takes place in him and in the visible universe.

As Man recognises the controller of creation he understands himself. He admits his body must not only be a place of peace, but must also be healthy also. Accepting the individualised self in all its effulgence dwells in him, Man realises he is instead identified with the three outer bodies [physical-astral-causal]. His spiritual journey is obstructed. With an unhealthy body, an uncontrolled emotion-ridden mind and an unenlightened causal personality or *chitta,* he is disabled.

The human body has the ability to heal itself. Unless abused over a great period of time, Man agrees to healing with energising and healing exercises. The body abused for over two decades is so filled with stress and temptation that it refuses transformation. Chronic habits of ignoring a body's wisdom need an increased time period to heal. This is often denied to Man.

Cosmic Awareness is a powerful enlivening source filled with *prana.* It far surpasses the power of the human mind. Man can channel this creative *pranic* energy and induce healing in his body through the healer's willpower, concentration, faith, reason and common sense. Healing is also possible through the transfer of enlivening energy from evolved astral beings to mortals on earth.

Diseases, especially chronic diseases, are deeply rooted in the subconscious mind. A trained healer must devote to positive affirmations made to a patient's subconscious mind. Until he reaches the super-conscious causal mind, healing is not possible. Here the mysterious powers of cure stay in Man's unconsciousness. These need awakening. Diseased habits of the subconscious must be uprooted by deeper and repeated efforts at affirmation and meditation for healing.

The Laws of Nature must be obeyed. Unbridled desire, fear, rage, intolerance, greed and overindulgence cause bodily disharmony. Cultivating peace and faith frees the mind from disturbing thoughts that trigger disease, decay and death. These mental cures are superior to physical cures. Will, imagination, faith and reason are all states of awareness. They allow Man to act through them from within. Internal instruments cannot understand the effects of energisation or transformation of body cells. Man cannot recognise the supreme healing Self, unless the healer and patient make himself worthy. Through self-discipline, sages enter His *[Purusha* or Consciousness] and Her *[Prakriti* or Awareness] domain to appeal for remedy.

The subject of psychic **healing crisis** merits discussion. Many have experienced this already and many more will trail after. It is an experience, an outcome that simulates an illness. It is often triggered by a healthy act, which is both naturally and nutritionally sound. Fasting, refraining from stimulants, eating natural food for a few days, meeting an advanced spiritual soul or solitude and intense meditation for prolonged periods have been created situations gone awry. The discomfort of a healing crisis can be intense, especially when the seeker does not pay heed to his body's needs before embarking on prolonged meditation. A selective, proper diet of fresh fruits and vegetables or a bout of fasting, whichever applicable, is recommended as a cure.

Truth

There are as many paths to Truth as there are stars, but one needs to follow the one that speeds up spiritual evolution. A lot is written and a lot is said about spirituality. But few take any action. Unless one prompts such progress, one cannot make out the Self.

Learning spirituality from books is like learning to drive without a driving instructor. Truth is learned from a realised *guru* who has experienced the Self in his own being. He is able to define the seeker's self, and, at the same time, show him the layers of ignorance under which the soul is hidden. A *guru* is a repository of wisdom. He is unrestricted even as he lives in the body. The serving *guru* does not incur the effects of his outward, worldly actions, because he worships in service. He promotes Nature purely for his love of Her. He delivers expecting nothing. He renounces his action of facility and relinquishes its effects. The Law of Cause-Effect does not touch such a teacher. The effect is felt in the Cosmic Mind for a Common Good. Civilisation is the beneficiary. A seeker is fortunate if he receives the grace of a *guru* who endures a seeker with worldly tendencies.

Many schools of philosophy consider Truth a relative quantity, with no value. But without awakening the faculty of intuition, the seeker can't unveil the Truth. A *guru* of divine realisation, however, has learned to balance the rigidity of the intellect and the fluidity of intuition. He can make out the truthful course of action in the different circumstances of the relative world. He judges from the point of the Absolute Truth. Many Masters have repeatedly defined Truth as they have personally experienced it. Their conclusions have always been the one and the same.

Everyone has experienced intuitive glimpses of inner feeling or conviction. They have proved right. However, this power of knowing is heightened through meditation and calmness. Over time this condition matures into pure intuition. A *kriya yogi* who knows how to withdraw his awareness and life force from the body of senses can enter the inner world of revelations. Here he receives knowledge emanating from the seven holy altars of the spine and the brain. Inner opinions are realisations. They come about as word-thoughts or distinctive intuitive feelings. Concentrating on these sources of power, the *yogi* hears the vibratory variations of the sacred sound AUM. And from within its sound-matrix, he hears, realises and experiences the supreme Truth.

Searching for the Truth is constant and continuous. Spiritual practice is not a pastime for certain minutes or hours. It is a constant awareness. It leads to a deep realisation that Man is the skilled architect and Supreme Self is the creator of this expression.

If Man is born of a want for self-manifestation, he must learn how he came to be. The seeker must learn about who modelled Man. To reach the depth of this Truth, he must become aware, first about his incoming breath. Until he knows this power, Man is unable to meet himself. Until this becomes an intimate experience for him, the Truth is still far away.

Fire of Knowledge

Every person can be freed of old habits and *vasanas*. They normally express themselves through the five outgoing senses and the five lower spinal *chakras*. The mind is preoccupied with desire. Energy is wasted in extrovert activity. The ruling deity of extrovert existence is the Law of Cause and Effect *[karma]*, the Law of Qualities *[gunas]*, not to mention the Law of Relativity *[raaga-dvesha]*. All are supplementary to the weight of *karma*.

Man exists in ignorance or *avidya*. He is unaware that he is provoked by the play of *Maya* expressed as Nature's luring qualities. The five spinal *chakras* suffer the agitation of insatiable wants, potent anger, unquenchable greed, eager possessiveness and overbearing pride. Creative *Maya* further fuels restlessness of breath and thoughts. The drama is played out through three nerve channels or *nadis*. The *tamasic ida* exerts inertia. *Rajasic pingala* is restless for action. The central *sattvic sushumna* hankers for harmony. Pulled in all directions, Man lives an agitated existence.

From birth to death the untutored Man lives and dies unaccompanied by any understanding. Then, one day he is told about breath. He is taught to discipline breath. It becomes the only known method to free him of intellectual delusion. Through this, he meets a realised teacher. He teaches Man to transcend nerve channels or *nadis*.

The seeker is taught to **Meditate** and it provides him insight. This **Knowledge** carries him to the formless introverted state of stillness and silence, above the pituitary. He is taught to determine real from unreal. He understands change from *changelessness*. He moves away from where the unenlightened *chitta* personality lives. He authenticates mind and intellect are veiled by ego. He moves away from where he previously surveyed his life. He has reached **Renunciation.** Man discovers he once used the entire universe as his personal playground for self-indulgence.

He makes extended effort at meditation. By self-healing he seeks to correct whatever was, or is, unbalanced in him. Intuition gained through meditation ignites to burn ignorance. Like a blazing fire it cleans the lower centres in the spinal cord. The mind engrossed in, and preoccupied with, materialism rethinks life.

The seeker regains his composure. He is in Renunciation. By withdrawing his senses into his self he restores balance within himself. He renews and refashions his dealing with society and with Prakriti or Creation. The inner voice of intuition knows the right answers. **Tranquillity** guides the seeker with what to say, how to act and how to move.

However, the seeker must listen only to this compelling life force. It takes him exactly where he needs to go happily. He desires alignment with the Mother's Plan for a Collective Good. The seeker's body, mind, intellect, emotions and *vasanas* together become a singular path. **Steadiness** and **Happiness** allow obedience to all three Laws of Expression *[karma, gunas, raaga-dvesha]*. These changes are recorded in every cell. *Prana* or life force mediates such changes in the DNA. The Centre of Awareness in the thalamus, above the pituitary *[ajna chakra]*, aligns with Cosmic Memory.

It is this intuitive knowledge, born of intense meditation that burns ignorance or *avidya*. As the mind withdraws from the five lower centres and senses, steadiness replaces agitation. By withdrawing above the pituitary, want and ambition are destroyed in the fire of wisdom. Here, the seeker sees the Cosmic Vision of *Prakriti* and hears the Cosmic Vibration of AUM within and without. The witnessing Man is still and silent. He feels the breath until *swasayama* becomes *pranayama*. In the fire of *prana* he is One with the Cosmic Spirit.

The sum total of this sequence in meditation is a changed awareness. It compels the seeker to take the Spiritual Path.

He sees objects, emotions and thoughts [OET] with a different mindfulness. Meditation is Man's return journey to Nature's lap, its constituency represented in the thalamus. And having made the necessary changes in the divine cave, the seeker adjusts with Nature as well. Man, now, serves Her.

By freeing the *ida* and *pingala,* the *sushumna* in the spinal cord is cleared. The mind cancels restlessness of desire and is put to rest. The seeker takes his awareness towards the pituitary, and above, for gradual enlightenment. As the individualistic self or *chitta* ignites old ways in the fire of intuitive knowledge, he undergoes self-unfoldment and Self-realisation. As the mind leaves the worldly domain and rises above the pituitary, Man enters the lap of Nature. This is the domain of super consciousness, where She frees Man from the three worldly Laws of Nature. Man, aware that he spent a lifetime seeking materialistic wealth, knows he has reached spiritual wealth. Finally, the direction of his human existence is being served through meditation.

The Past

Seekers on the Path of Meditation often get stuck at this level. This happens because of Man's preoccupation with remorsefulness for sins of a previous life. Seekers, who are unable to forgive themselves, *block* themselves here. Man's harbouring something against others also hinders his progress. He projects learned images, programmed into his psyche, and on to the people he meets. Constantly playing childish games of vengeance, he displays need to punish others. False or misled religious notions by dogmatic religious people also obstruct the seeker at the *kutastha*. Creating roadblocks at the *ajna chakra* is risky. Instead of climbing the *ajna,* seekers sidetrack into the unnatural. Instead of evolution there is regression.

Old memories of many antecedent births have the ability of confining us in the past. They become our own natural reservoir of past habits and opinions. But the Self is beyond the mind. Our endeavours should, therefore, be directed at becoming the Self. By responding to Collective Conscious Self in the present, Man stops projecting back into the past, or into the future.

There are no shortcuts to meditating deeply. The unenlightened *chitta* must be transcended. And even if achieved, a Self-realised master instils true understanding of the gradual self-unfoldment. The spinal field is a jungle of extrovert inclinations. *Karma, gunas* and *raaga-dvesha* govern it. The forest must be cleared and seeded with new thoughts that allow the mind to rise above restlessness. All the *nadis* of the spinal cord must be cleared from the *sushumna,* so awareness can rise unobstructed towards the *ajna chakra* and beyond.

A disciplined lifestyle ensures an intelligent use of the senses. Breath control ensures the seeker develops purity of personality *[chitta]*. Constantly watching the inspiratory breath, being pulled automatically by the Self into the *ajna*, reminds the seeker of the gift of life as His Grace. Every action performed by Man is also because of the life-giving power of *prana* that energises and enlivens the biological body. Such awareness frees the seeker of ego and restlessness and his mind and intellect rise above the pituitary. He develops a sense of detachment from worldly inclination. From this understanding, the *chitta* personality watches the twenty-four material elements at play through the biological body and the world.

Affirmation

A spiritual aspirant has a million questions and many doubts. Even a sincere seeker is often tempted to desert the battlefields of spiritual life. Man usually seeks God in the heavens *above.* He is convinced He is not in Man's perishable body.

With this thought, he moves along a path of repetitive mistakes. The journey that leaves him mentally restless and physically unhealthy is of bewilderment. This restiveness continues until he meets a sincere teacher. Although awarded with boundless grace, nobody except a teacher can remove the doubts of delusion from Man's life.

He is, at first, taught to seek God's presence in the constantly changing universe. Man begins to see Him in the stars, the sky, flowers and the seed. Having identified Him in plants, birds, creatures he sees Him in Man.

Then, Man is made to see That beyond all change and in the changeless Soul of the Universe. This is *secret knowledge.* It is seen and understood only through intuitive divine vision. And this information is powerful. The teacher then draws Man to the knowledge that God is not outside, but inside him. He shows him where to find the Soul above his eyes. Self-unfoldment is an integral part of his education in Soul Culture.

The meditating seeker makes a discovery. His incalculable wants are fulfilled with the divine experience of the Cosmic Vision in the *kutastha.* Still, the teacher encourages him to advance slowly along the same slippery spiritual pathway. As the seeker's love and dedication for the teacher grows, it gives him the faith to walk the rest of the way.

As he moves up the lower centres, moving northwards to the *sahasrahara* in the brain, his inner awareness is sequentially purified. His senses and sense organs, spontaneously, become well reorganized. He becomes fit to travel the rest of the way. The journey takes Man beyond his body, mind and intellect. In a spirit of complete surrender, the seeker allows his teacher to take him to the next step. He is in the dominion of a transformed life of pure Soul Culture.

The ultimate vision of being One is difficult to grasp without continuous practice. The seeker frees him from drowsiness and sleep. He spends more time in meditation, day and night, until he reaches his goal. He cannot bear to forget the Lord while asleep and while awake. His awareness is with Him with every breath. He makes a conclusion. There is a changeless presence behind the constantly changing, metamorphosing creation of the past, present and future. He accepts the Universe is the Lord with a form. He swears He is also of a formless Infinite.

He affirms that he, the seeker, is this infinite creation. Through the inner eye of intuition and illumination, he experiences himself as vast and infinite. The more he practices inwardly to fix his attention into the space above the pituitary, the more he walks the path of gradual self-unfoldment and eventual Self-realisation.

With awareness fixed into the space above the pituitary and *looking* into the Cosmic Vision, the brilliant light of a thousand suns is revealed to him. It is a soothing light of pure Awareness in his own inner sky. The devoted seeker melts as he hears the constant sound of the original word. He penetrates the sound to reach its origin, and having risen above his mind, intellect and ego, he dissolves into the womb of both Awareness [Matter or *Prakriti*] and Consciousness [Spirit or *Purusha*].

Of course, these experiences have to be explained. Being with an experienced teacher ensures the seeker earns Soul Culture through self-analysis. For he has, after all, been given only a glimpse of the Universe.

Divine Illumination

By repeatedly entering the inner sky through meditation, the seeker enters the *kutastha* opposite the *ajna chakra* above the pituitary. Here, in the space between the pituitary and the *sahasrahara,* is the place of pure awareness in the *thalamus,* where he makes out the divine illumination of the spiritual eye, which some call the *Third Eye.* It is the *kutastha chaitanya.*

This spiritual eye is the single eye of intuition and omnipresent view in the *Kutastha Chaitanya* or Krishna-Christ Centre of Universal Intelligence. It can be seen only with an inner gaze, while focusing at the divine cave, between and behind the eyebrows.

> The light of the body is the eye: if therefore thine eye be single, thy whole body shall be full of light.
>
> MATTHEW 6:22.

A deeply meditating seeker *sees* the eye as a ring of whitish golden energy of **AUM.** It encircles an inner deepening blue *pranic* life force of **Tat.** In its brightened causal centre of Truth is the five-pointed white star of **Sat.**

To see this eye is like witnessing a million suns, moons and stars simultaneously. This is the formless, all-pervading, brilliant Divine Illumination of the Cosmic Being. It makes the seeker realise His greatness, within and without.

The spiritual eye is the gateway into the supreme state of divine consciousness in *Samadhi* or the state of One. As he enters the spiritual eye, the seeker experiences super-consciousness in *Samadhi.* It is an unearthly joy of Soul-Spirit realisation, of the Soul being One with the AUM of Cosmic Intelligence in all Creation.

> No man cometh unto the Father, but by me [the son or any prophet or Krishna-Christ Consciousness]
>
> JOHN 14:6

Through the spiritual eye's central star of the *kutastha*, the yogi sails his Awareness into the omnipresence of Cosmic Consciousness, while hearing AUM. And while merging with the divine sound of infinite waters, and vibrations of Light and Energy, Man enters constituents of Creation.

Aum Tat Sat

Section VI

Figures

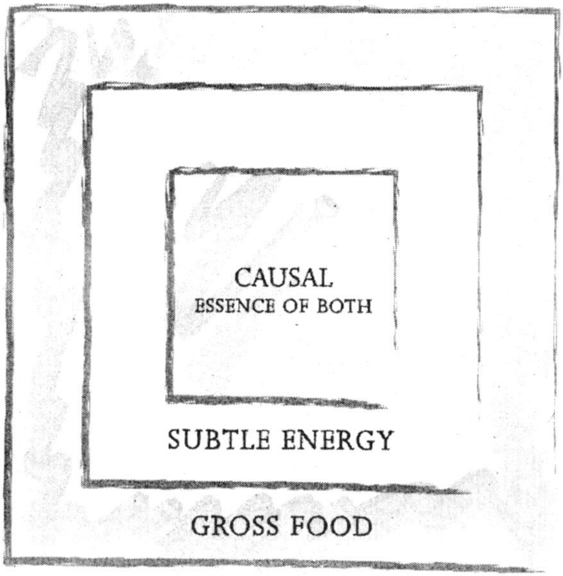

Figure I: The Three Bodies

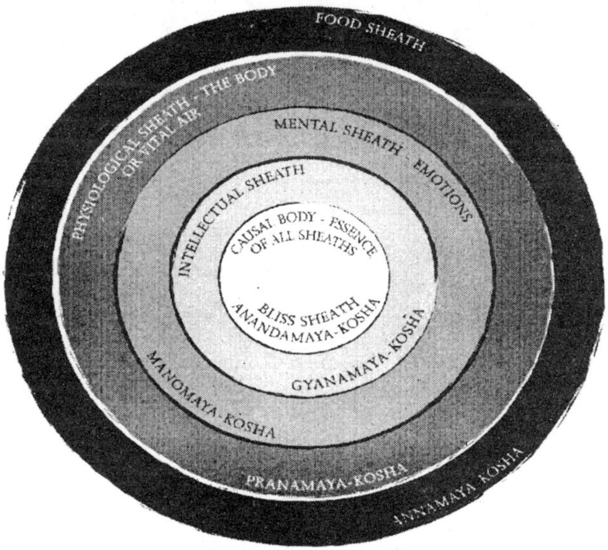

Figure II: Five Sheaths

The Food and Physiological Sheaths make up the Gross Body, in the ego's 'Waker' state. The Mental and Intellectual Sheaths make up the Subtle Body, in the ego's 'Dreamer' state. The Bliss Sheath, the Essence, makes up the Causal Body, in the ego's 'Deep Sleep' state.

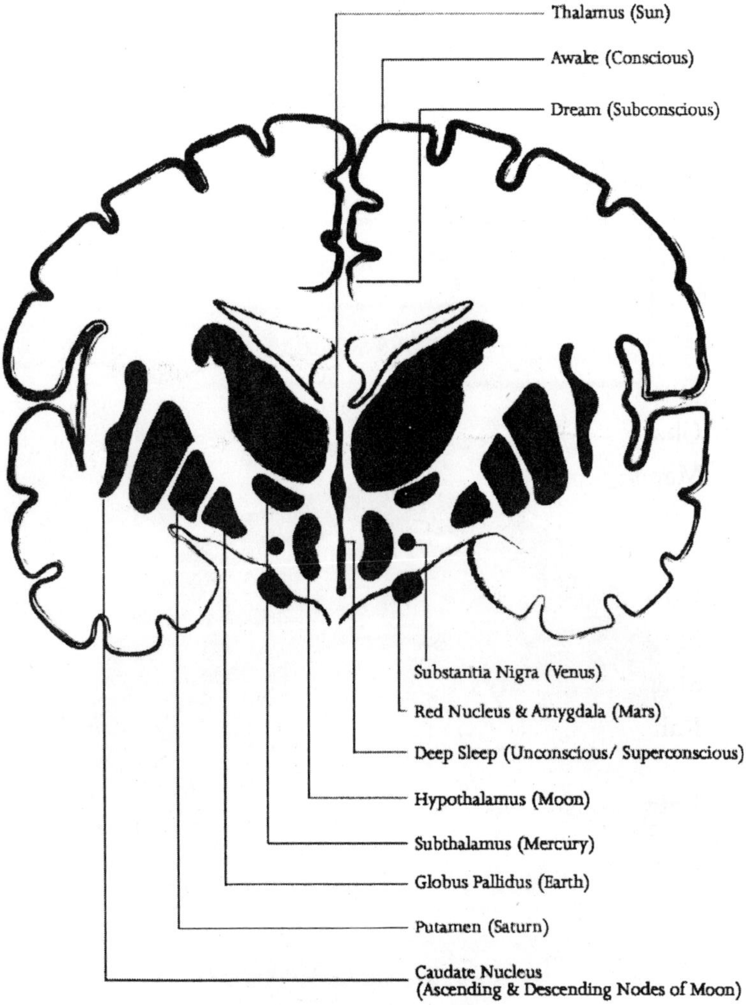

Figure III: Universe in the Brain

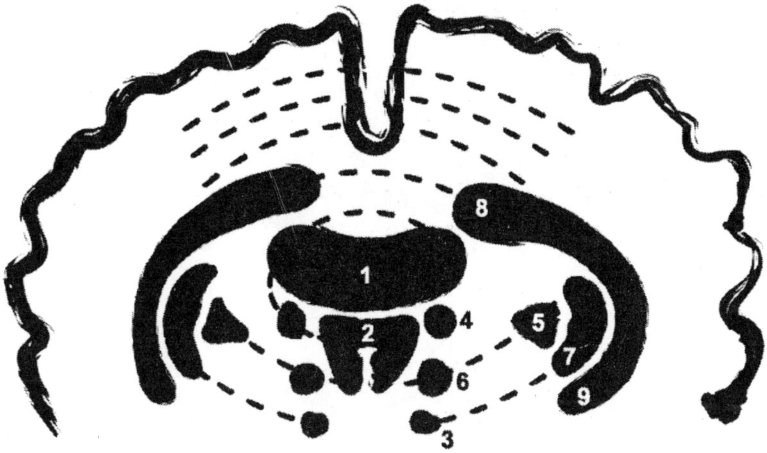

Figure IV: Planets Influence Man...

1	Surya (SUN)	=	Thalamus
2	Chandra (MOON)	=	Hypothalamus
3	Mangal (MARS)	=	Red Nucleus + Amaygdala
4	Budha (MERCURY)	=	Subthalamus
5	Guru (JUPITER)	=	Globus Pallidus
6	Shukra (VENUS)	=	Substantia Nigra
7	Shani (SATURN)	=	Putamen
8	Rahu (ASCENDING NODE)	=	Caudate Nucleus Head
9	Ketu (DESCENDING NODE)	=	Caudate Nucleus Tail

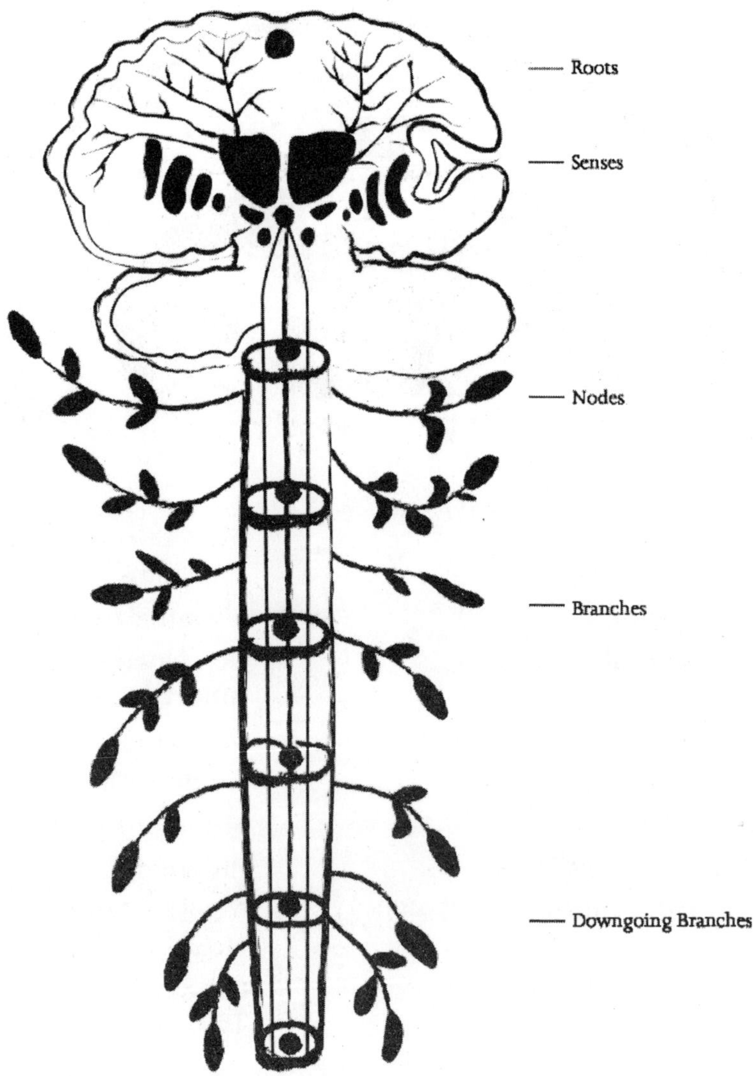

Figure V: Ashwatha Tree (The Upside-Down Tree)

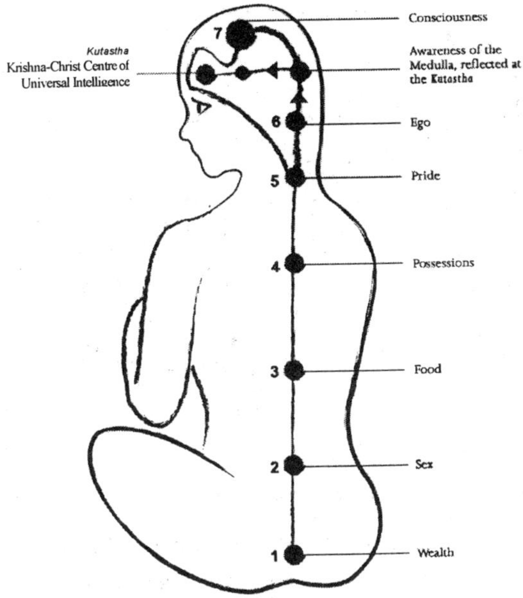

Figure VI: Centres of Activity

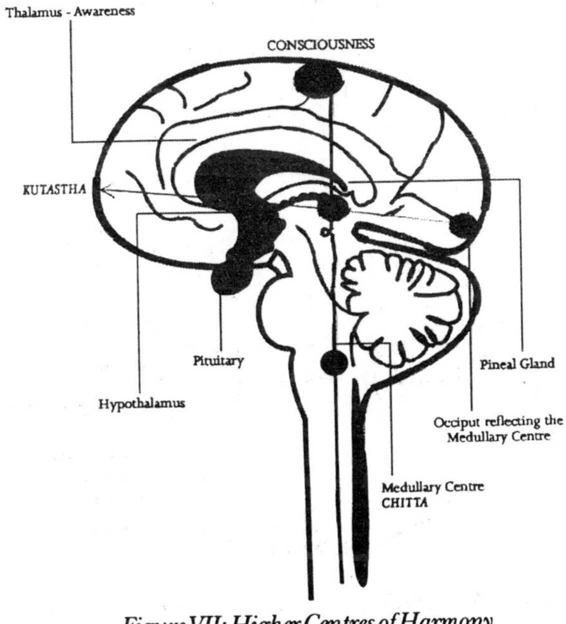

Figure VII: Higher Centres of Harmony

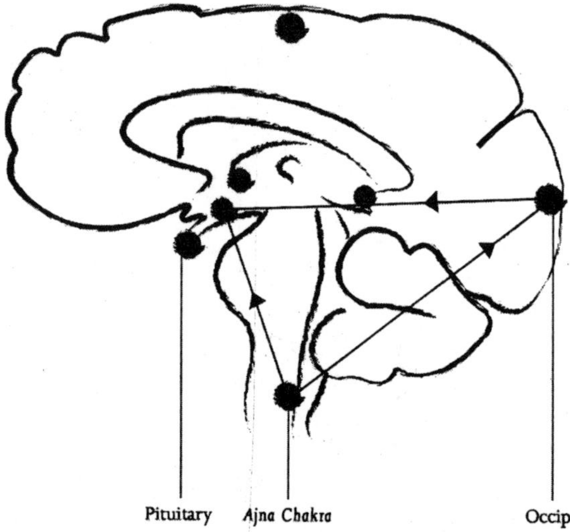

Figure VIII: Ajna Chakra reflected as Third Eye

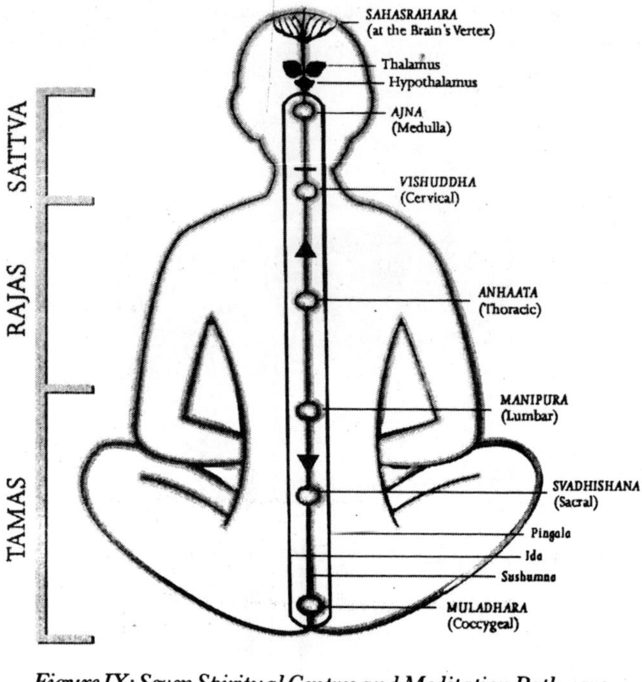

Figure IX: Seven Spiritual Centres and Meditation Pathways

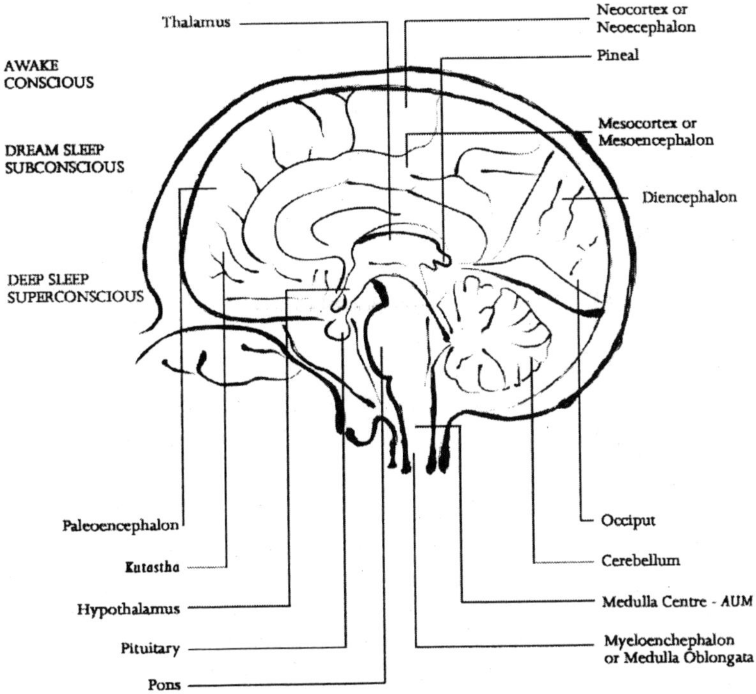

Figure X: The Level of Awareness–Consciousness

BOOKS OF RELATED INTEREST FROM NAB

9 SECRETS OF SUCCESSFUL MEDITATION— *Samprasad Vinod*

The author brings a fresh approach to Meditation; he inspires his readers to experience Meditation and to integrate it with their daily living; only those who really enjoy Meditation will do it regularly and thus get the most benefit from it. He shows the reader how to develop a true taste for Meditation, to take pleasure in it and thus to trigger spiritual growth and harmony in daily living.

ISBN: 978-81-7822-137-3

EXPLORING MEDITATION: Master the Ancient Art of Relaxation and Enlightenment— *Susan G. Shumsky*

This spiritual self-help book offers easy, step-by-step procedures to master the ancient arts of meditation and enlightenment. It offers practical techniques to increase love, power, and energy; reduce stress and tension; improve health; reverse ageing; and bring well-being, and peace of mind to everyday life. This book demystifies abstract concepts and provides a road map to the inner life, leading beginners safely through the maze of the spiritual path, pointing out signposts and pitfalls along the way.

ISBN: 978-81-7822-296-7

GETTING TO WHERE YOU ARE: The Life of Meditation—*Steven Harrison*

This book is written not as one more how-to book but to dispel the notion that there is some technique of meditation that will solve our problems, relax our bodies, and bring us to the radiant light of truth in twenty minutes a day. Meditation is about everything. We are already doing it, effortlessly. It is our natural state of existence. This book is as much about what meditation is *not* as it is about what meditation *is.*

ISBN: 978-81-7822-202-8

MEDITATION WITHOUT GURUS: A Guide to the Heart of Practice—*Clark Strand*

This book strips the practice down to its essential heart—simplicity, lightness and peace—showing you that the most important part of practice is not whether you can get in the full lotus position, but rather your ability to become fully present in the moment. Encouraging and inspiring, this one-of-a-kind guide provides the frame-work to make meditation a joy—not a fearsome, rigid choice.

ISBN: 978-81-7822-242-4

KARMA AND CHAOS: New and Collected Essays on Vipassana Meditation— *Paul R. Fleischman*

In eight poetic and inspiring essays Dr. Fleischman explores the interface between psychiatry, science and meditation. This book may open your heart to the well-springs of love and compassion, wisdom and equanimity available to all who develop a deep understanding of the experience of impermanence. This book is intended to inspire people on the path of Vipassana Meditation. The therapeutic benefits of self-awareness have never been more needed than in our complex world today.

ISBN: 978-81-7822-177-9

THE MEDITATION HANDBOOK: Meditations to make Our Life Happy and Meaningful— *Geshe Kelsang Gyatso*

This book makes you aware and deepens your insight about—What is meditation and how it works, how to integrate meditation into our daily life and how to find lasting peace and happiness through meditation. The book provides essential background material on meditation—why we need to meditate, how to prepare for meditation, and how to enjoy a successful meditation session. It teaches twenty-one easy-to-follow meditations. By following them we can transform our mind, fulfil our true human potential, and find lasting peace and happiness.

ISBN: 978-81-7822-066-6